DIVINE REVELATION OF THE RAPTURE

Jesus Christ warns of the world collapsing on the day of the Rapture. Holy Spirit reveals how Christians will be taken. "Enter into a relationship with Me" or be left behind, says the Lord.

Anthony Dovkants

Brazil

2024

Divine Revelation of The Rapture

Anthony Dylan Faria Dovkants

1st edition – June of 2024

Direction Anthony Dovkants

Coordination Rogério Araújo

Review Rogério Araújo and Carla Tavares

Graphic design and diagramming Carla Tavares

Cover Carla Tavares

Index

	Dedication	4
	About the author	5
	Introduction	6
Chapter 1 -	Billions will soon disappear in the blink of an eye	10
Chapter 2 -	The Day of The Rapture	25
Chapter 3 -	The Fire of God, The Glory of the Heavenly Father, and the Glory of God the Son	36
Chapter 4 -	Where do we go? Origin and destination	46
Chapter 5 -	The warnings and timing of the Rapture	65
Chapter 6 -	Noah and my father	79
Chapter 7 -	The antichrist is here, what should we do?	110
Chapter 8 -	Planning for the journey and living a life worth living	116
Chapter 9 -	Jesus is coming but the Father will also be upset	128
Chapter 10 -	Jesus Christ's Final Warning	146

Dedication

I would like to dedicate this book to our Heavenly Father, who loved me first, to Jesus Christ, who has my back, never gave up on me and rescued me so many times, and the Holy Spirit, who formed me, nurtures me, directs me and is with me everywhere I go. I love you Adonai Elohim.

Secondly, I would like to dedicate this book to my darling wife Ana, whose heart is generous and enduring, to my children Dylan Laurence, Stephanie, Jasmyne and Chloe, who are all blessings from the Lord and are His, to my father Keith, who has long been my inspiration and is central to the timing of the Rapture, and to my relentless mother Zaida, who prayed for me for so long to return to the Lord after becoming an atheist in my teenage years. Mother, a million times thank you for persevering. And lastly but not least, my darling little sister Dulcibella, whom I love dearly but have seen so little in her early formative years but hope to make up for that soon.

I would like to give a special thanks to Pastor Rogerio, who is my pastor and my mentor and whom I have fondly nicknamed Yoda and draw much inspiration from. And lastly my mother-in-law Pastor Clemilda, who is a source of encouragement and a rock, who the Lord put in my life.

About the Author

Passionate about the Lord, Anthony is a pastor at Christ-centric Holy Spirit-led Atmosfera Revival Church in Osasco, a city of deep contrasts with nearly 750,000 inhabitants in Brazil. He looks after the ministry of Evangelization at the church. Anthony has a repentant and undivided heart, this is what he prays for. He walks with the Lord, communes daily with the Holy Spirit in fellowship and seeks to do what the Lord asks Him out of obedience to God the Father's will.

His ministry is on the streets, in a supermarket, pharmacy, taxi, Uber, restaurant, a cinema, or outside or inside his house – in short, wherever God the Spirit, the Spirit of the Heavenly Father and the Spirit of Christ, deems best. Almost daily, Anthony talks to those who are baptized but no longer have a church and are lost. Every encounter is an opportunity to reveal what Christ wants for their lives before He comes back. Anthony's goal is to live every day to the most in Christ, to be a husband to his wife and a father to his children, be a son to his parents and increasingly grow spiritually in His grace, praying and using the gifts the Lord has given Him.

Introduction

The Lord gives us visions to change the world. This book is about what the Lord God revealed to me in a dream about the Rapture on June 12, 2023. Since that night, Jesus Christ put it into my heart to share with others what He will do on the last day of the Church on earth, an event that will impact every man, woman and child. Indeed, Jesus Christ through the Holy Spirit told me:

"The people must know the message that I have given them… time is short and the time is now."

For this reason, I have endeavored with this book and trust that it helps you to understand what is to come and how to prepare. For this work contains encouragement from our Lord God as well as warnings. I do not add or take from them. For I have sought to squeeze out every possible truth from the vision that the Holy Spirit gave me to help readers understand how the end will happen for all Christians, whether they are or are not in a relationship with God the Son.

If anything, this process of understanding the vision has been like putting together an intricate jigsaw puzzle, often ascertaining its veracity by cross-referencing verses across the Old and New Testaments. This analysis included talking to fellow pastors, consulting theologians as well as eschatological texts and praying to the Lord in the Spirit over the period of nearly a year.

And the conclusion of it all? The time is coming when the Rapture will finally happen in our lifetimes. I have seen our final moment on earth before the Lord takes us up into the sky. It is going to be a glorious day for our triune Lord God - God the Father, God the Son and God the Spirit.

However, for those who are not lifted up to the heavens and are left behind, it will be a terrible day. Christ confirms the aftermath of the Rapture at the end of this book, stating quite bluntly, the world "*will collapse*" in the wake of this event. His message came to me when the work was nearly finished.

So, I urge you dear reader, please tell others about the Lord God's message for this book was written in the Holy Spirit, so spread the word, the days are counted before Jesus Christ returns. Until then, keep the faith that Jesus Christ died for our sins and live in relationship with Him, urge others to fix their eyes and thoughts on Him, for Revival and the Rapture are coming.

On a separate point, please note dear reader, that whenever we read, hear or watch something about God, we must ask ourselves in what spirit was the work conducted and executed. Is this very book *Divine Revelation of the Rapture* from a false prophet, who is nothing more than a wolf in sheep's clothing and whose sole intent is to confuse and spread lies about Jesus Christ? Indeed, how should we approach this book as a reader? Is it just a work of foolishness, a fantasy, or worse yet crazy fiction?

Or is it a book that reveals a truth that has come from our Lord God and heralds the single most important moment in history since the resurrection of Jesus Christ and that it will happen in our lifetimes?

To know the truth of the book, you as a reader must ask yourself in what spirit this work was written and question its accuracy. This is important to me and should be important to you when you read this work, which is to me a revelation from the Lord God. To understand better the spirit of this book, let's look at 1 John 4 where the Apostle sets a clear parameter on how we should tackle and read *Divine Revelation of the Rapture*:

"[1]Dear friends, do not believe every spirit, but test the spirits to see whether they are from God, because many false prophets have gone out into the world. [2] This is how you can recognize the Spirit of God: Every spirit that acknowledges that Jesus Christ has come in the flesh is from God, [3]but every spirit that does not acknowledge Jesus is not from God. This is the spirit of the antichrist, which you have heard is coming and even now is already in the world (1 John 4:1-3)."

So how do we test this work and know if it is real? Follow the book's revelations and arguments and see whether they recognize the Spirit of God and acknowledge that Jesus Christ is the Son of God and that all of this is the will of God the Father.

If that does not happen, then this work is from the spirit of the antichrist. Simple, right? So, before you read this work, pray to ask the Holy Spirit to guide you so that you can know whether the words on these pages reflect or not the will of God the Father and glorify the Son. I leave this to you to decide but allow me this one last comment for my heart is taken and I confess that I am not impartial on the matter.

My goal is to reveal the glory of God the Son, the living Jesus Christ, and consequently the glory of God the Father (John 17:1-5) through the Rapture event, and also show how I arrived at the conclusion that the vision presented by the Holy Spirit is *very* real and that the time is coming for the living in Christ to be transformed and go to the sky.

For Jesus is coming back and nothing can change that. Indeed, it is important to note that this conclusion was reached before Christ's message came to me about the horrors of a post-Rapture world and why no one can afford to be left behind.

Consequently, we must all take heed and be in a relationship with the Lord if we are to be raptured and finally know (personally experience) our permanent home with God the Father and God the Son in the sky. For we will soon go to the Kingdom of God, a kingdom that is built on eternal foundations where we will know of no pain, illness, depression or death.

However, while I am excited to be able to reveal to you this vision from the Lord, the revelation from the Holy Spirit does come with warnings that I urge readers to heed, for all of God's children must prepare for the greatest and fastest journey of their lives. And this all comes as the world is currently being prepared to worship the antichrist. So, until that great moment of the Rapture, we must all fix our eyes, stay steadfast in our belief, get closer to the Lord and focus on Jesus Christ, the Risen and Living Son of God:

"[1]Therefore, since we are surrounded by such a great cloud of witnesses, let us throw off everything that hinders and the sin that so easily entangles. And let us run with perseverance the race marked out for us, [2]fixing our eyes on Jesus, the pioneer and perfecter of faith (Hebrews 12:2)."

God bless and see you up there in the sky if we do not meet beforehand in this life! Until then, *"come, Lord Jesus,"* and that *"the grace of the Lord Jesus be with you all. Amen."* To Him, who loves us all.

Chapter 1
Billions will soon disappear in the blink of an eye

"The time is now! The Kingdom of God is near! Repent, and keep believing the gospel (the Good News) (Mark 1:15 ISV)!"

In the name of Jesus Christ of Nazareth, everything that will be revealed is for the glory of the Heavenly Father and His one and only begotten and risen Son. Indeed, what you are about to read affects every man, woman and child on this planet, and by this I mean the Rapture - the final and culminating moment of the Holy Spirit's perfect and completed work in the Church, involving everyone who is in a relationship with Jesus and affecting everybody else who is left behind on the planet.

The Rapture is the moment when billions will be lifted up to the sky and will disappear from the face of earth in an instant. More than one billion souls will be children under the age of 13 alone (UNICEF 2023 data[1]). The rest will come from the world's current Christian population of nearly 2.4 billion. The Rapture is prophesied in multiple verses (1 Thessalonians 4:16-17, 2 Thessalonians 2:1, 1 Corinthians 15:51-52, Philippians 3:20-21, 1 Corinthians 1:8, 2 Corinthians 5:1-9), and we will explore some of them in greater detail later.

It is critical to note that this book will detail the second most important event in the history of the world since our Lord Jesus Christ, God the Son and perfecter of faith, went to the Cross for our sins, rose on the third day and then spoke to hundreds of witnesses about the Kingdom of God for 40 days before ascending to heaven to be seated by the right hand of God the Father.

Indeed, the Rapture is coming and what will soon be revealed in this work directly affects the last minute of every man and woman in Christ and all children on this planet - whether they are in Christ or not.

This moment, which will happen in the blink of an eye, will confirm the imminence of *Parousia*, the second coming of our Lord Jesus Christ – a moment that will send lovers of this world into mourning (Matthew 24:30 NIV) when *"they see the Son of Man coming on the clouds of heaven, with power and great glory."*

Following a dream from the Holy Spirit during the early morning of June 12, 2023, this book will detail who will be taken and why, how we will be taken, where we will be taken (origin and destination) as well as provide insight as to when. That does not mean I am going to tell you the year, month, week or hour - for no one knows when the Rapture, Tribulation and Second Coming will happen. Certainly not!

That said, the Lord God did reveal in the vision several clues about the timing of the Rapture because He wants us to be prepared (Amos 3:7), really prepared for the greatest journey in our lives for when we will be irreversibly transformed and lifted up to the sky.

And if you are an unbeliever or an unchurched Christian, who is not in a relationship with Christ, may the Lord have mercy on your soul because the consequences of being left behind on the day of the Rapture are going to be terrible (as revealed at the end of this book).

In short, time is running out for that moment when billions will suddenly disappear. This isn't scaremongering or sensationalism. The Rapture is one of the many End Times signs that were revealed by Old Testament and New Testament prophets alike. Such prophecies are either already fulfilled, being fulfilled or will soon be fulfilled – for Christ has revealed that the signs will all occur during the same generation.

One of the many obvious signs that is being confirmed is the implanting of microchips in the right hand so that people can buy goods in supermarkets. This is starting to happen in China and in the US as unsuspecting folk start to get onto this digital cyborg bandwagon.

Some may think it is cool, many will not, for there will come a day when the implanting of such a chip will become mandatory for everybody on the planet, according to Revelation 13:16-17. Why is this chip or mark as it is described in the Bible so important?

People will be forced to have the chip implant because it is the mark of the Beast. Folk will either unwittingly or knowingly have the chip implanted.

"[16] It also forced all people, great and small, rich and poor, free and slave, to receive a mark on their right hands or on their foreheads, [17] so that they could not buy or sell unless they had the mark, which is the name of the beast or the number of its name (Revelation 13:16-17 NIV)."

This is just one of many signs that is starting to be fulfilled, however, let's get back to the Rapture and explain some of the basics.

So, what is the Rapture? Before proceeding with the vision of the Rapture that the Holy Spirit revealed to me, it is important to understand the two stages of the Rapture already detailed by Paul the Apostle in 1 Thessalonians 4:16-4:17 – especially if you are fuzzy on the basic details or are still struggling to believe that it will happen.

"[16] For the Lord himself will come down from heaven, with a loud command, with the voice of the archangel and with the trumpet call of God, and the dead in Christ will rise first. [17] After that, we who are still alive and are left will be caught up together with them in the clouds to meet the Lord in the air. And so we will be with the Lord forever (1 Thessalonians 4:16-17 NIV)."

It seems incredible to believe that the dead will be raised from their graves and the living will be transformed, and that both will be lifted up to the sky to be with our triune Lord God forever. But is it so farfetched? No, not really, not at all.

It is important to know that Jesus has already shown that this is not only possible but that He has already blazed this trail for all of us. Let's retrace the basic steps of the Rapture by seeing what Jesus did nearly 2,000 years ago! Christ the Redeemer died for our sins on the Cross, He rose on the third day and 40 days after that He ascended to heaven to be seated at the right hand of our Lord God.

In short, Jesus died, His body was placed in a tomb, but He came back to life and afterward went up to the sky. Christ has completed the Rapture circuit of death, resurrection, and ascension. These are the three core elements that involve the Rapture. Christ not only did this to show He is God and that death is beaten but to demonstrate to all Christians that those who are dead will be resurrected!

For Christ "*is the beginning and the firstborn among the dead (1 Colossians 1:18).*" You see, the Lord has already paved the way to the Father! He is the exodus of salvation and the Way of Holiness (Isaiah 35:8). We can more than hope, we can know that the dead in Christ will not only be resurrected but the living in Christ will for sure be transformed and taken up to the sky.

Jesus has already shown us that the Rapture is not only glaringly possible by tracing His final steps on earth, but the risen and living Son of God has also demonstrated that the Rapture is not a question of if it will happen but a question of when it will take place.

Indeed, Ezekiel was treated to such a vision detailed in chapter 37 of his book when the Lord asked him to prophesy to "dry bones," in fact, a *"great many bones on the floor of the valley, bones that were very dry (Ezekiel 37:2 NIV)."*

The chapter is quite a spectacle to behold as God graphically shows how the *"bones came together… tendons and flesh appeared on them and skin covered them, but there was no breath in them."* Ezekiel was then asked to prophesy to the breath:

> *"[9] Then he said to me, "Prophesy to the breath; prophesy, son of man, and say to it, 'This is what the Sovereign LORD says: Come, breath, from the four winds and breathe into these slain, that they may live.'" [10] So I prophesied as he commanded me, and breath entered them; they came to life and stood up on their feet—a vast army (Ezekiel 37:9-10 NIV)."*

This chapter is a depiction of the resurrection of the dead as well as the restoration of the house of Israel, however, it provides a clear insight into what will happen when those in Christ will be awakened from their graves and taken up on that last day of the church on earth (1 Thessalonians 4:16).

It is interesting to note that William Shakespeare, a devout Christian who frequently used Biblical references in his works and would have known of the verses in Ezekiel 37 and 1 Thessalonians 4, had the following written on his grave:

"Good friend, for Jesus' sake forbear, to dig the dust enclosed here. Blessed be the man that spares these stones. And cursed be he that moves my bones."

It is also curious to read that an archaeologist claimed that Shakespeare's skull was likely missing from his grave, according to a Reuters report March 24, 2016. Has it gone? Did someone dig it up? Does it matter in terms of the Rapture?

No, not at all. For the Lord will provide, for the bones of many Christians have long turned to dust. This is all important to contextualize as Jesus was raised on the third day, when his bones and body were still intact, however, the Lord does not need a body or bones to bring people back from the dead when we remember that our Lord God made humanity from dust in the first place (Genesis 2:7, 3:19).

So, we should not worry about our dear departed dead, for our Sovereign Lord is the God of the impossible (Matthew 19:26). Moreover, our Lord God will not raise a headless Shakespeare, for we would be limiting our faith in the Father to the point of heresy, and I am pretty sure England's favorite bard would appreciate such an outcome either as his mind is surely the finest part of him.

Apologies, for anyone who knows me, my English humor and sense of irony is often misplaced, and this book is first and foremost about 1 Thessalonians 4:17, the living who will be lifted up and not the dead, whose resurrection is detailed in Ezekiel 37.

What can we expect to happen in the wake of the Rapture? Whether we like it or not, understand it or not, the Rapture will not only mark the end of the Church and the disappearance of billions of people, it will come before the Great Tribulation, a period when Satan's prophet will be given authority to rule the world for 42 months (Revelation 13:5).

It will be a terrible time for those who are left behind by the Rapture. First of all, the global economy will collapse and parents, who are left behind, will despair across the world as they try to understand why their children suddenly and inexplicably disappeared.

Remember the outcry in Egypt after the 10th and final plague took the lives of the firstborn to free the Israelites (Exodus 11-12)? Can you imagine the chaos across the world after a billion-odd children vanish in the blink of an eye for the Lord will take His children back, they are His and no one else's. And what about those who are left behind to pick up the pieces?

Among them will be unbelievers and spiritually-dead unchurched (out of relationship) Christians – those who were baptized but lived a life of disbelief and next to zero relationship in the Lord. All who are left behind will be subjected to Satan's rule through his prophet, who is currently moving the chess pieces around as he directs the steps of Hamas in the Gaza strip and Middle East. Indeed, all of those who are left behind after the Rapture will be forced to worship the Beast.

So, should we be worried? Yes, absolutely, if you are one of those left behind. The post-Rapture world will be a place of mourning, loss, unchecked sexual permissiveness, murder, adultery, theft and economic collapse, while demonic oppression will run riot with demons out in the open.

We are already starting to see this phenomenon as the world is being prepared for their arrival. And the lost (those who are left behind) will then be led to worship the antichrist or face death. I cannot imagine how horrible it will be except to say that the Lord revealed the horrors of this post-Rapture day before finishing the book, so read on to find out more as we have not yet arrived at the part of the vision!

So, if you are someone who does not believe in Christ, keep reading because this book represents an opportunity to know the Lord. If you are a Christian, who no longer goes to church and has no relationship with the Lord (praying once in a while is not what Jesus wants from us), yes you should be worried because the Lord is calling you back right now – stop losing the spiritual battle and letting the enemy rule your life (whether you are aware of this or not), get back to church and let the Lord transform you by faith in Christ!

To clarify this point further, it is important to know that we must all fix our eyes and thoughts on the Lord Jesus Christ of Nazareth (Hebrews 12:2) for there is salvation, healing and deliverance in His powerful and wonderful name. This must come first in our hearts before we heed the warnings from our Lord God about the Rapture itself.

For this book will detail our Lord God's sovereign will for us and His three clear warnings around the Rapture that go beyond what is typically preached about preparing for the end.

So in part, this book is more than a calling to be ready, it is more than a calling to buckle up for the ride, it is more than a calling to be wary of the signs, it is a calling to be in Christ today, to be in a relationship or to get back into a relationship with the Lord this day, it is a calling to change our priorities today and live a life that is worth living because Revival is coming and the Lord is intent on bringing His people home to Him and the Father.

For those mired in despair, depression and rejection, the Lord is going change all that towards the end. Jesus is coming to gather all of His people and He is going to do wonderful things through the Holy Spirit during Revival.

It will be unmistakable to miss! Soon, the people will know in their hearts and minds that our Lord God is there for them, He has always been there for them and He will be there for them right up to the last millisecond before His glory descends and raises us all up. Amen?

So why is the Rapture going to happen? To cut straight to the chase, the Rapture is for the glory of Jesus, it is the completion of Christ's work on the Cross in our time, for He will personally take us up to the sky in a blaze of His loving Fire of God by the power of the Holy Spirit. The Rapture also represents the completion of the Holy Spirit's work with the Church.

On top of this, Jesus is removing us from the land for our own protection and this is why the Rapture is going to happen. The Rapture is to spare true believers in Christ of the very worst that is to come from the Great Tribulation. It is deliverance, pure and simple on a God-sized scale. We are to be spared of the horrors of the Great Tribulation thanks to the Lord's even greater mercy and grace.

This is a huge deal and I am grateful for this. For those who have read the prophecies from the Old Testament and New Testament prophets, the end of this age is to make way for Christ's millennial reign before the Kingdom of God will come down from the sky and we will all be with the Father and the Son for eternity. Before that happens, the world will undergo total wipeout on the day of the Lord, when He will effectively press the delete button to make way for new creation.

"10 But the day of the Lord will come like a thief. The heavens will disappear with a roar; the elements will be destroyed by fire, and the earth and everything done in it will be laid bare. 11 Since everything will be destroyed in this way, what kind of people ought you to be? You ought to live holy and godly lives 12 as you look forward to the day of God and speed its coming. That day will bring about the destruction of the heavens by fire, and the elements will melt in the heat. 13 But in keeping with his promise we are looking forward to a new heaven and a new earth, where righteousness dwells (2 Peter 3:10-11)."

Thankfully the Rapture will spare us of all of that cataclysmic destruction as well as the Great Tribulation. Indeed, this is the point of the Rapture, to save us from the worst of what is to come. And it is worth noting that this is not the first time the Lord has rescued His people from calamity.

Lot and his family were extracted from Sodom and Gomorrah (Genesis 19) just before it was pounded to the ground by our Lord God's wrath.

"24 Then the LORD rained down burning sulfur on Sodom and Gomorrah—from the LORD out of the heavens (Genesis 19:24 NIV)."

Did you see it? The Lord rained down from the Lord in the heavens. God the Son was with Lot and his family, taking them to safety, while God the Father rained down sulfur from the heavens through the power of the Holy Spirit. The Lord saves. Christ saves. He is the Rock, who saves and comes to save, and He will do it time and time again.

However, we cannot be complacent about this, we cannot adopt the same attitude as that of Lot's sons-in-law, who thought their father-in-law was joking when he said:

"Hurry and get out of this place, because the Lord is about to destroy the city (Sodom and Gomorrah, Genesis 19:14)!"

Unlike Lot's sons-in-law, we cannot be aloof to the Rapture. Such an attitude will prove fatal and this will upset the Lord greatly. Our Lord God also did this with Noah when He gave him the means to build an ark of salvation ahead of the flood (Genesis 6-7, 2 Peter 2:4-9).

For us, or rather for those living in Jesus Christ of Nazareth, it will be no different. Once we are lifted up and transformed on the day of the Rapture, we will be purposefully removed from the global stage and will never know the worst of the Great Tribulation.

Lot and Noah are two examples of deliverance that Peter uses but we do not need to go to the Bible for such examples, for our Lord God is saving people from sending themselves to hell on a daily basis by delivering them from their own foolish stubbornness or wickedness.

Thirdly, and importantly, Jesus is taking us home, to our permanent home, to eventually be with Him in the Kingdom of God (Revelation 21-22, Isaiah 66:22-23), to live in the presence of our Lord God where there will be no more sin, tears, sadness, illness, poverty, death or oppression.

The Church and her members – the people of God, are to be spared the worst of the Great Tribulation and reconciled with the Lord! What a glorious day that will be for we should look to the Rapture as the great deliverance, as the Lord's final and greatest rescue mission.

Ok, but I am an unbeliever, I do not believe in Jesus but do not like the devil either, what should I do? Now, if you are an unbeliever reading this text and are worried about the Rapture, I need to tell you this, it is prophesied in the Old Testament and the New Testament, it is very real, I have seen it and I can tell you this, it is going to happen really fast and only those in a relationship in Christ will be raptured.

The rest will be left behind and what a cruel fate that will be. Christ is not a religion, He is the single most important relationship in anyone's life – ever.

And if you are tired of trying to do things your way, tired of thinking that life is not working out for you, tired of seeing things going wrong, tired of reacting to everything like a dog returning to his vomit, tired of horrible relationships, tired of oppression, tired of despair and depression, tired of wanting to die and not knowing where you are going, tired of trying different religions that do not work, tired of living a life without meaning, tired of living for your sins, tired of loving your sins, tired of just being you, tired of hearing your own voice in your life, and that you have absolutely no desire to worship the devil, then you must appropriate Christ in your life.

Why? Our Heavenly Father demands that we all pay for all of our sins, and such payment is with blood, and it can *only* be paid with holy, blameless, sinless blood, and the only sinless and blameless person who ever lived is Jesus Christ.

But why does it have to be this way? We cannot be in the presence of our Lord God or even get to heaven, or ever enter the Kingdom of God unless we too become righteous, blameless, holy and are forgiven (freed/redeemed) of our sins.

This is why our Lord God Jesus Christ of Nazareth came down from the throne to earth and made that payment in our place. He took our place on the Cross, He went and paid for our sins by going to the Cross and sacrificing Himself in our place with His holy, blameless and sinless blood.

Christ went to the Cross as the perfect sacrifice, like a lamb to the slaughter (Isaiah 53:7), He died for all of our sins and is the living Son of God. He paid the price so we do not have to, He redeemed us, for He is the only way to salvation and by accepting Christ in our hearts by faith, we are saved. There is no other way.

We cannot be saved by our own self-righteousness, we cannot buy a ticket to heaven or the Kingdom of God either, we cannot negotiate or barter our way in with charity. If you are a billionaire, your money is worthless. It cannot buy entry into eternal paradise.

For the gift of salvation is for free and only available to those who are ready to say, "Jesus died for my sins, Jesus is the risen son of God, Jesus is my Savior and Lord." No self-saving efforts or living for the self can get you in, and as disappointing as this may sound to those who hold to a more pluralist view (for they lean on their own human understanding), Jesus is the only way, truth and life.

No one comes to the Father except through Christ (John 14:6). Jesus made it so simple so that no one can get confused on this point. So, if you are at a crossroads or a quandary in your life, avoid spiritual death traps and let go of arguments such as why does God allow evil in the world, or I love my sins.

Why sell yourself out so cheaply? Instead, open your heart and do not worry about your life filled with sin today, that should not stop you from accepting Christ, for the Lord will change the way you live tomorrow, He will change your habits, who you are and what you like in such a gentle and gradual way that if you pursue an ever-deepening relationship in Him, you will find yourself gladly walking away from who you once were.

In short, Jesus is the key to opening the door to the Kingdom of God in your life and starting eternity, yes eternity, for the second we are baptized, we start eternity in Christ. For Jesus came so that *all of us* have a chance to get home, to get back to the Heavenly Father, to be reconciled with our Lord God and live with Him forever (literally, this means never-ending time in the Bible).

This is the Good News. We are saved. Jesus is the ark of salvation, indeed, He is leading the Exodus of salvation because Christ is the salvation, He is the Good Shepherd and the door, and we are the last days Exodus.

For God the Father is our loving and doting parent, and like any parent, He wants us to live with Him and love Him in the same way that He loves us. For the Lord God loves us just as much as He loves God the Son, and this is why Jesus was able to go to the Cross out of immeasurable love.

He did this because our Lord God in turn promised Jesus a people, His people to save and for one day, for all of us, for all of the generations since Adam and Eve, to come together and live and reign with the Heavenly Father and Jesus in the Kingdom of God.

For God the Son has given us a way to get to New Jerusalem, the Kingdom of God, we need only accept Christ by faith, to accept that Jesus died for our sins on the Cross and then enter into a relationship with Him as well as start to lead a life that is morally pleasing to the Heavenly Father.

When we do this, we will start to change and begin a new journey, for we are reborn in Christ. And this is the point. This is what our Heavenly Father wants – for us to become more like Christ, for when we accept God the Son as our Lord and Savior, the Father no longer sees us but sees the Son in us.

This is how we become righteous and perfect in God the Father's eyes. This is how we are made perfect and once baptized we have a lifetime of working on our holiness by becoming more and more like Christ.

"For by one sacrifice he has made perfect forever those who are being made holy (Hebrews 10:14 NIV)."

By living in a relationship in Christ, the Holy Spirit can do His complete and perfect work in us. This is what Adonai Elohim wants from all of us – He wants us to come to Him so that He can transform us into His likeness and become like Christ for we are all being prepared for an age that we do not yet know but will soon know post-Rapture.

However, it is important to note that we cannot change and become like Christ because we ourselves can change ourselves. Our own will is finite in terms of energy and staying power. We cannot maintain a diet for years, let alone months or weeks by our own sheer willpower.

By our Lord God's grace, love and infinite patience through the Holy Spirit, we are able to reach new heights and become new creatures in Christ. This is why when we are baptized, the Lord sends the Holy Spirit to enter us, make a home in our hearts and take us to new heights by helping us lead a new life in Christ that is worth living.

So, if you are an unbeliever, meditate on all of this, ask the Lord to talk to your heart, pray, open a Bible and keep reading this book and expect the Lord to answer you. I know He will touch your heart.

Now, if you are a struggling or doubting Christian, in and out of your relationship with Jesus Christ, in and out of churches, in and out of spiritual habits, keep praying, keep reading the Bible, keep going to a church that connects you with Jesus, for our Lord God loves you, our Lord God wants you to do His will for your life and hear His good, pleasing and perfect will for your life.

It is also important to learn to pray the Breath Prayer (Come Holy Spirit…) daily, commune with the Holy Spirit and seek Him – with time you will come to know Him more and more (I recommend Peter Scazerro's excellent Emotionally Healthy Spirituality Day by Day, which helps Christians move closer to the Lord, transform and develop their ability to hear Him in their lives).

We must never give up, we must keep praying for a repentant and undivided heart, keep seeking Jesus and reading the Bible too and ask ourselves what does the Lord God want from us this day, week, month, year or decade?

Seek His will and remember the Holy Spirit, the Spirit of Christ, the Spirit of Peace, will take care of the rest and bridge the gaps in a way that only a perfect parent knows how when his child stumbles or is struggling.

Remember how the Lord God transformed Moses into the greatest of all prophets in the Old Testament? Remember how Moses kept complaining that he was no great speaker, he was not eloquent, and that he was simply not up to the task of freeing the Lord's people from Pharoah's grip? Our Lord God wants to transform all of us without exception.

So, what should we expect to happen between now and the Rapture? For Adonai Elohim, our triune Lord God, God the Father, God the Son, and God the Spirit, is calling His people to come to Him before it is too late. The Lord God wants His people to return to the churches now and reconnect with Him in prayer, community, and service before it is too late.

Relationship is a key aspect of salvation, and it is of little coincidence that the Lord's calling right now is for the unchurched (the baptized who roam the earth like unbelievers) to return to the Church and revive their relationship with our Lord Jesus Christ.

If you are one of those who has either left the church or is a believer but is weighed down by sin, then know this, no sin is too great for our Lord Jesus to forgive. Confess and go back to the church, do not be distracted by Netflix, Instagram and anything else that takes you away from knowing our Lord God's love and will for you, for the Heavenly Father wants us all to live in a relationship with Him and pursue a life that morally pleases Him during the course of the remaining years before Christ returns.

Indeed, if you are reading this text, it is because the Lord God guided you to it and He wants you to know that He loves you, He wants you to know what will happen at the end so that you can prepare, tell others about what is to come, live a life that is worth living and ensure that we all live each day to its fullness in Christ.

And if you are in a relationship with the Lord, then keep seeking, keep knocking, keep praying, keep deepening your relationship in Him so that you can grow and know His good, pleasing and perfect will for your life.

For He wants so much more for us than we could possibly imagine, He wants us to become like Christ above all, He wants us to reach new heights and to keep scaling higher, to run the good race and finish it well by faith in Christ.

To do this He gives us supernatural gifts too so that we can hear His voice in our life and bring others to Christ through miracles. Can you hear Him talking? Do you know how? Do you know of our Lord God's great love for you? We will come to this later.

But before we move on, let's address the elephant in the room – the antichrist. He is already among us. That was revealed on two separate occasions by the Holy Spirit after the Rapture vision. The antichrist will be explained later but fear not, Jesus Christ has the keys to Hades and death itself.

There is power in His Name and He will protect us – for He has always protected us whether we realize this or not. This truth is infinitely more important to Christians today (knowing that Christ has our backs) than figuring out who the antichrist is.

For our Lord is greater than Satan, and we should not act in a hapless way, thinking that we are defeated. We overcome in Christ, we are victors, we are eternal royalty, and this will become clear once we all reach the Kingdom of God on the day of the Rapture.

Lastly, it is crucial that we realize that we are part of the last generation to walk this earth in Christ, yes, we are part of the last generation of the Church, the last generation of Christ's body and the last generation of humanity. Our Lord God describes this last generation as the Noah generation, the only generation that happens twice in the history of mankind. More of this to come later!

Chapter 2
The Day of The Rapture

[17] After that, we who are still alive and are left will be caught up together with them in the clouds to meet the Lord in the air. And so we will be with the Lord forever (1 Thessalonians 4:16-17)."

On Sunday June 11, 2023, the night before the dream on the early morning of June 12, I asked the Sovereign Lord to give me a prophecy before I went to sleep. This was not the first time I had prayed for this. It must have been around the third time that I had asked on occasion.

You see, I wanted to have a vision or in this case a Holy Spirit-revealed dream. I yearned to see heaven, to learn or experience something about Jesus. I didn't have anything in mind at all, except that deep down in my heart I wanted the Lord to pull back the curtain of heaven just like the Holy Spirit did with Peter in Acts 10:9-23, when the Apostle saw heaven in a vision and all manner of different *"four-footed animals as well as reptiles and birds (Acts 10:12 NIV)."*

Another great example is when John the Apostle was exiled on the island of Patmos and he had a vision of Christ (Revelation 1:9-18), and *"among the lampstands was someone like a son of man, dressed in a robe reaching down to his feet and with a golden sash around his chest. [14] The hair on his head was white like wool, as white as snow, and his eyes were like blazing fire (Revelation 1:13-14 NIV)."*

The thing is, I always want to know more about Jesus and experience Him in a real way. I always desire to take my relationship with God to another level – I am sure many seek the same. Do you? Maybe, the Lord had planted this seed in me by giving me the heart that He gave, I couldn't be sure because I have always wanted more from Him, to learn more and increase my knowledge as His servant for service.

Plus, I think the gift of prophecy is wonderful. Used correctly, the gift will edify any church or Christian (1 Corinthians 14:4). I always marvel at those who speak in tongues, prophesy and are used by the Lord.

What sublime gifts He has given us to do His work and mission by submitting to His divine authority and obeying Him. When we reveal His will for others and pray in the Spirit for deliverance, for example, depression or suicidal tendencies can be rapidly quashed.

It is beautiful to see when the Lord brings deliverance to a person whose life had come to halt, only to see their eyes light up and suddenly everything restarts again.

It is little wonder that Paul the Apostle held the gift of prophecy in such high esteem, it is a powerful weapon of evangelism and re-evangelism (1 Corinthians 14:1-5).

"Follow the way of love and eagerly desire gifts of the Spirit, especially prophecy. ²For anyone who speaks in a tongue[a] does not speak to people but to God… ⁴Anyone who speaks in a tongue edifies themselves, but the one who prophesies edifies the church (1 Corinthians 14:1-2, 4 NIV)."

Secondly, I had always been impressed when Peter cited the prophet Joel (Joel 2:28-32) and said that God will pour out His Spirit on all people in the last days, sons and daughters will prophesy, young men will see visions, old men will dream dreams and servants – both men and women, will also prophesy (Acts 2:17-21).

What impressed on me the most was Peter's use of the words last days. Peter quoted Joel's verses to a crowd during Pentecost in Jerusalem. In his mind, he was living the last days. Indeed, first century Christian Jews felt that Jesus would return during their lifetimes.

For me, the use of the words *"last days"* in Acts 2:17 also stuck in my mind, and I had already wondered are we not there yet? And not just this, in verse 18, it states, *"even on my servants, both men and women, I will pour out my Spirit in those days."*

Today, I know that "*those days*" are here and we will visit this theme in a later chapter about the timing of the Rapture and how we can be sure that we are in the last hour of our Lord God's clock!

So, I prayed that Sunday night as I confessed to myself that I was tired of dreaming futile dreams about the world. Such dreams had become inconsequential to me because I could never remember anything the next day anyway.

As I closed my eyes that night, little did I know that what the Lord was about to reveal would affect every man, woman and child in the world. That night, the Holy Spirit revealed the will of God the Father for the world and the glory of God the Son.

This is what the Sovereign Lord showed me in a dream that Brazilian wintry night and please read it as if I were sitting in front of you, telling you exactly what I saw and didn't see, explaining what I heard and didn't hear, adding hindsight commentary along the way! This is what I saw:

"I was on my cellphone with my father in what appeared to be my office. I was aware of a desk and a chair but I couldn't see either. I merely sensed the presence of office furniture. I was next to a window, standing, holding my smartphone and I clearly sensed that there was also a family on the other side of the room. I couldn't tell who they were, I couldn't see who they were. I tried to make them out, to see their faces, what they wore, something or anything at least, but it was a blur.

The Lord didn't let me see their faces. I thought one of the people was my wife, and I vividly remembered trying to insert my wife into the dream, but she was removed. It seemed an odd moment, almost awkward, the way she was taken out. I thought it was my dream.

It was at that point that I realized it wasn't. In a way, the removal of my wife from the dream was tantamount to interference on my part. Instead, I took a step back and on some level understood that I was there to watch and not get involved, so I decided to go with the flow of the vision.

In short, no one from my family was there but I had sensed that at the very least there was a woman and child on the other side of my office. As I tried to understand my surroundings, I saw myself talking to someone on my cellphone.

"Confess your sins to Jesus," I told my father. "Confess your sins to Jesus," I repeated. I don't know how I knew that I was talking to my father at the time, for I couldn't hear what he was saying on the phone, in fact, I couldn't hear anything during the vision except for my own voice, but I just knew that I was talking to my father.

This is important for I witnessed the whole vision in utter silence. I didn't hear what the family on the other side of the room said either.

As I spoke to my father, I had this strong feeling that the Rapture was about to happen, that I was about to be taken. As I pleaded with my father – at least that is how I felt on the cellphone, I noticed outside of the window a wall in an adjacent building or possibly a wall that was part of the same building.

The wall had no windows whatsoever. It was whitish in color, it was wide but more importantly very tall. I couldn't recognize where I was in fact. I couldn't see where I was, in what building, house or other structure but I sensed I was in some kind of church.

As soon as I had noticed the wall, its color, height and lack of windows, I suddenly saw a bright orange light reflecting on the wall. In fact, there were two types of lights, one was a dark, rich and beautiful orange, much like the amber light you see on the back of cars.

The other light was yellow but much lighter, brighter, radiating. The bright yellowish white light radiated in thin shimmering lines in between the much thicker and beautiful amber lines. I was captivated by the lights outside. They were beautiful.

I had never seen such a phenomenon before. The strong and bright orange colors were shimmering or flicking just like the blue and almost white lights that we see reflecting on a wall next to a swimming pool. The light was beautiful, peaceful and mesmerizing. I was only able to see exactly what I was looking at – there was no greater peripheral awareness.

Instead, everything else was blurred out of my field of vision. Normally, we are always aware of our surroundings but to me in this vision they were purposefully blurred. I was only allowed to see what I was allowed to see, nothing more or less.

As I looked at the light, I felt it was promising me something that was about to come. However, the bright lights just disappeared, and suddenly I was enveloped by a very profound sense of disappointment that it had gone away.

I felt at a loss, as if I had lost someone special in my life. I could not even begin to describe the loss but as I tried to process this feeling, the intense dismay was also accompanied by a feeling that the Rapture was no longer going to happen.

I then saw myself again by the window, continuing to stand and listen to my father on the phone but I don't know what he said. I could not hear any noise at all, not even the noise of those who were around me in the room at the time, they just remained in the background. Suddenly, I interrupted my father:

"It is now," I said, "it is now," I repeated urgently, as a sudden feeling of the very imminent Rapture took a hold of my whole being again.

At this point, I had no sense of time itself, but as soon as I had said "it is now" to my father for the second time, a bright strong orange light, an amber light just like the one that I had seen on the wall but without any thin lines of gleaming whitish yellow, descended from the sky right in front of my eyes, it occupied all of my vision, it radiated all around me, it surrounded me and as fast as it had come down, I felt a jolt as I was lifted up.

The jolt was akin to that feeling when you are driving your car quickly and you suddenly go over a drop or dip in the road, or that jolt when a rollercoaster car or train starts to move.

As soon as I felt the jolt, my chest and stomach sank into my body and then I saw myself looking down on where I was once standing, it was like a blur, I was being lifted up, I was looking at myself at a height of 4 meters high and I saw where I was previously standing.

The office could no longer be seen, I was within the amber light, and as soon as I realized this, I was moving at such incredible speed that within the next moment, I found myself in some kind of palatial space, filled with whitish-grey shining walls and precious stones.

The gems were shimmering in the light, which was coming in from somewhere, but I saw no windows either. It was as if the precious stones had their own light. It was at this point that I noticed that the family that I had sensed back in my office was in fact Brazilian.

I knew who they were because I knew they were Brazilian but I was not allowed to recognize them, let alone see them. I just knew them and do not know how I knew them either. I also noticed that I no longer had a cellphone in my hands. As I tried to understand where I was, the vision just ended."

I woke up, and for the first time in my life, I immediately thanked God for what I believed to be a vision from Him. I whispered into my pillow, thanking Him. It seemed the most natural and logical thing to do for I quickly concluded that I had just witnessed a dream from the Lord but for some reason I just went back to sleep, thinking one thing only, "Anthony don't forget what you saw, write it down in the morning."

That next morning, for the first time in more than a decade, I was able to remember every detail of my dream. This is important. Normally, I automatically forget what I had dreamed the night before. I am mentally incapable of remembering a dream from the night before. It is as if my memory does an automatic memory dump every morning. My dreams are futile in content and substance.

That all said, I was skeptical the next morning, I didn't really believe what I saw, and more importantly, I didn't understand what I had witnessed either. I immediately discarded the vison.

I had thanked the Lord for the dream right after it had finished but I could not contain my skepticism that next morning. Could this really be a vision from the Lord? Am I going nuts? I had been praying for prophecy and had I finally received one?

At this point in my ministry, I had not yet received the gift of prophecy because I had not yet started to speak in tongues – that did not happen until October 2023 – so I really did not understand what was going on.

For the next few days, I did what I didn't expect to do, and anyone who knows me, would not have expected me to do either, I went quiet, and running in silent mode, I pondered every aspect of the dream.

I really didn't grasp what it was that I saw, however, questions abounded, what was that orange light? What was that building with the tall whitish wall? Where was I up in the sky? Where was Jesus in all of this? Was I really raptured? And what about my imagination, could I have made this all up?

I had to look at this from a clinical, theological and intellectual standpoint, I needed to come to terms with what I saw through analysis and reason and not anything that my heart was telling me, for my gut said, "yes, it is true, you were raptured."

Having grown up on Baker Street, I felt I had a mystery on my hands that needed to be solved, however, no detective could give me the answers I was looking for. I needed divine interpretation, spiritual support, teaching and guidance from the Holy Spirit and from those filled with the Holy Spirit.

Only those from our Lord God could help shed light on the matter, for you must be of the Spirit to understand matters of the Holy Spirit. For those who are not in God the Spirit will think of all of this as mere foolishness and cannot understand what is written, heard or spoken because such things are discerned only through the Spirit.

"The person without the Spirit does not accept the things that come from the Spirit of God but considers them foolishness, and cannot understand them because they are discerned only through the Spirit (1 Corinthians 2:14 NIV)."

This includes the dream that I had. Therefore, if you are reading this book and you are in the Holy Spirit or considering Jesus as your savior, then let the Spirit speak to your heart as you read on but remember approach this subject of the Rapture like Luke did when he analytically considered as a doctor the truth of Jesus Christ, the virgin birth, the Good News, the Cross and eternal life in the presence of the Lord.

Approach this text analytically, and like Luke, who was a doctor, diagnose this singular moment in future human history from the standpoint of an open heart and mind, allowing the Holy Spirit to talk to you and guide you – for God the Spirit guides us into all truths that reveal Jesus Christ (John 16:13)!

For we are all urged to examine and cross-examine the Christian faith before we make the most important decision in our lives – to accept Christ or not. Christianity is not based on closing our eyes and hoping for the best just because others already know in their hearts who Jesus is.

We must all come to Christ on a certain intellectual level with open hearts until we reach a certain point where the Holy Spirit bridges the gap and takes us to the other side, revealing Jesus Christ and removing our spiritual blindness, convicting us of our sins and bringing us to our knees in repentance as we start to grasp His divine holiness. By doing so, we do the will of the Heavenly Father, who chose us before the foundations of the world were set in place. For He wants all of His children to be reconciled to Him and live with Him, holy and blameless in His sight:

"For he chose us in him before the creation of the world to be holy and blameless in his sight (Ephesians 1:4 NIV)."

So in the same way that we are all urged to investigate the truth as to whether Jesus Christ is our sovereign Lord or not, I immediately approached the vision with deep skepticism as I sought to understand the veracity of the Lord's revelation, and determine whether in my own heart the vision had come from the Lord Jesus Christ himself or that it was part of my imagination, an elaborate hoax on myself, or worse yet, something from the enemy!

As before, I kept quiet for three to four days before I turned to Pastor Rogerio, a man unusually brimming with the Holy Spirit, and I told him what I saw. At the end, I confessed to him that I didn't understand all of the parts of the vision, that I thought it was from the Lord, but I didn't quite trust what I had seen and was concerned that I had imagined it.

At this point, I really felt blind, like there was a veil over my eyes and I needed someone to point me in the right direction. Pastor Rogerio was the first of four pastors to do so.

"It is all true, it is from the Holy Spirit," he said confidently and without hesitation. We were in June and I barely knew the pastor except that he prophesies, talks in tongues, occasionally prays prostrate before the altar, and is used daily by the Holy Spirit to bless others. I looked at him earnestly, hoping to hear more as I still remained skeptical about the dream.

Rogerio, whom I have since come to call Yoda because he is filled with the Holy Spirit and uses multiple gifts from the Lord for his ministry, surprised me with what he said next:

"Read the first nine chapters of Ezekiel to understand better the Fire of God," he said smiling. "Ok, I will," I said sheepishly. I knew I was being led to texts I had read in the past and was wondering what I could have missed.

"The whitish wall with no windows, you need someone who can interpret dreams to answer that part for you," he added, smiling. "Do you know who can do that?" I asked ironically, knowing full well that he was wanted to answer the question. "I can answer that for you. I can interpret dreams," he confirmed. I smiled back, I motioned with my hands as if to say "do tell."

"Well, the whitish wall is that of a church and the absence of windows means that it does not have any vanity," he added.
So, I had my first batch of clues and first confirmation. Firstly, the dream is about the Rapture. Secondly, it is going to happen in some church structure during the daytime.

From what has already been prophesized about my future ministry, I will at some point lead a church in the UK, possibly in London, and while I had always marveled at the centuries-old yet ageless elegance and splendor of the churches of England, it was clear to me that the future church that the Lord has already long planned for me will be in a modern building with a tall whitish wall with no windows. I look forward to moving in!

Thirdly, I also had a pointer as to the meaning of the lights that I saw in the vision – they were so remarkable and beautiful that I had to understand their significance.

I felt that I was starting to piece together parts of a much bigger puzzle involving the most important moment in the history of the Church since it was first established by the Holy Spirit at Pentecost when He descended upon 120 disciples and gave them the gift of talking in tongues.

The Holy Spirit came so that Jesus can be with us wherever we go through God the Spirit - the Spirit of Christ and the Spirit of the Father.

Now in a clear reversal through the Rapture, the Lord will soon take up his people so that we can be with Him for never-ending time, speaking His divine tongue and completing what is in effect a three-part saga that began when men tried to build the Tower of Babel to reach the heavens through their pride and forcing the Lord to end what was then blossoming into the creation of a one-world kingdom under the influence of a single tyrant.

This could not happen. So, our Lord God stepped in and confused the language of the "whole world," He scattered the sons and daughters of Noah "over all the earth," and consequently stopped them from "building the city" (Genesis 11:8-9 NIV).

Why did the Lord interrupt the building of the Tower of Babel? In verse 6 it states that the Lord said, *"if as one people speaking the same language they have begun to do this, then nothing they plan to do will be impossible for them."*

Moreover, the time had not yet come for the creation of a one world kingdom under a tyrant. That prospect has been reserved for the Great Tribulation when the enemy will have the authority over the earth for 42 months (Revelation 13:5). Thankfully we have the Rapture and will not have to deal with the Great Tribulation for who could bear such a time?

So, if this is all confusing, let's recap what we have understood until this point in its simplest form. In short, billions will disappear. There are two stages to the Rapture, the dead sleeping in Christ will rise from their graves and ascend to heaven, while those who are alive will be transformed and lifted up to meet the Lord in the sky. We must all be in a relationship with the Lord (the importance of this will be explained in greater detail later because it really matters).

What else do we know? The Rapture is about rescuing the Lord's people and sparing them of the worst of the Great Tribulation, which is marked by 42 months of the beast's rule over all of the peoples of earth.

The Rapture is also about taking us to our Lord God's permanent home (more to be revealed about that). And lastly, on a personal note, it will happen to me while I am in my office at church.

At this point, I felt more had to be investigated. There were still so many details yet to account for and understand about the Rapture – the single most important event since Jesus Christ's resurrection and ascension to heaven to sit by the right hand of our Heavenly Father.

Chapter 3
The Fire of God, The Glory of the Heavenly Father and the Glory of God the Son

"From what appeared to be his waist up, he looked like gleaming amber, flickering like a fire. And from his waist down, he looked like a burning flame, shining with splendor (Ezekiel 1:27 NLT)."

Following up on my talk with Pastor Rogerio and his pointers, I reread Ezekiel 1. When I reached verse 26, my eyes started to widen, by verse 27, my jaw was ajar, and when I slowly went over verse twice 28, I was jumping up and down like a schoolboy as if I had just discovered some never-before-seen treasure. I was looking at these verses in Ezekiel in a whole new light:

"[26] *Above this surface was something that looked like a throne made of blue lapis lazuli. And on this throne high above was a figure whose appearance resembled a man.* [27] *From what appeared to be his waist up, he looked like gleaming amber, flickering like a fire. And from his waist down, he looked like a burning flame, shining with splendor.* [28] *All around him was a glowing halo, like a rainbow shining in the clouds on a rainy day. This is what the glory of the LORD looked like to me. When I saw it, I fell face down on the ground, and I heard someone's voice speaking to me (Ezekiel 1:26-28 NLT).*"

These verses ram home what is for me at least the most important sign of the Holy Spirit's revelation of the Rapture, and that is the color of the Rapture itself and what this in turn represents, its weight, its true significance. You see the color is important because it is a key marker that helps us identify that the Rapture is imminent.

To understand the importance of the color of the Rapture itself and what it means, we need to understand the meaning, or rather the exegetical truth behind Ezekiel 1:26-28 and there is only one truth here.

In verse 26, we see *"on this throne high above was a figure whose appearance resembled a man."* This is Jesus Christ. For Jesus is the "anointed" yet "hidden one" in the Old Testament. He is also referred to as the Angel of the Lord or the Son of Man.

But how can we be sure it is Jesus? In Ezekiel, our Lord is revealed as just a *"figure."* Firstly, most academics state and agree that the book is about Ezekiel seeing a "vision of Yahweh as a God of judgment and hearing his commission as a prophet of judgment" (p.15 Word Biblical Commentary Volume 28, Ezekiel 1-19, Leslie C. Allen). Here is the thing, Yahweh is God the Father and God the Son (Genesis 19:24, Isaiah 44:24, Matthew 28:19, John 1:3, Colossians 1:16, John 8:58).

But what about Yahweh as a God of judgment? Is Christ that judge? *"In the presence of God and Christ Jesus, who will judge the living and the dead, in view of His appearing and His kingdom (2 Timothy 4:1 NIV)."*

Ok, but what about the God-man *"figure"* in Ezekiel's vision being seated on the throne? Could that be Jesus?

"Lord Jesus, after he had spoken to them, was taken up into heaven and sat down at the right hand of God (Mark 16:19 ESV)."

Here is the thing, Mark 16:19 states that Jesus sat down at the right hand of God and not on the throne of the Father. On top of this, Christ took His rightful place 40 days after the resurrection, which came nearly 600 years after the book of Ezekiel was written.

So, while Mark 16:19 establishes that Jesus clearly sat on a throne, it is clearly not the same as what is written in Ezekiel 1:26 because the figure in that verse was on a throne high above – and there was no mention of any other throne. So how can we be sure that it was Jesus in Ezekiel 1:26 because Mark established that God the Son sits at the right hand of God and it does not say that Christ sat on the Father's throne. That answer is in Revelation!

"The one who conquers, I will grant him to sit with me on my throne, as I also conquered and sat down with my Father on his throne (Revelation 3:21 ESV)." That solves that question about whether Jesus sits on the throne of the Father.

In short, what I am trying to establish here is that Jesus, God the Son, is separate and yet one with the Father. Remember in Genesis 19:24 NIV where it states that "*the LORD rained down burning sulfur on Sodom and Gomorrah—from the LORD out of the heavens"?* In Genesis, He is separate from the Father at that very moment but Christ is still one with Him as God the Son. Let's not forget that Christ is God.

Jesus said to them, "Truly, truly, I say to you before Abraham was, I am" (John 8:58 ESV).

So, why is it so important to the Rapture to establish that Ezekiel 1:26 is about Jesus? We need to understand that the figure high above on the throne is Jesus because in verse Ezekiel 1:27, it states: *"From what appeared to be his waist up, he looked like gleaming amber, flickering like a fire."*

This verse is critically important because it explains why the color of the lights matter so much to the vision of the Rapture! Bear with me, for I am building up to the significance of the Rapture. Remember in the previous chapter about the "two types of lights?" Let's recap: "One was a dark, rich and beautiful orange, much like the amber light you see on the back of cars. The other light was yellow but much lighter, brighter, radiating."

I must add that the Rapture lights were shimmering to me in a peaceful and graceful yet mesmerizing movement. I have always found a flickering flame graceful and hypnotic to look at – just to help explain that further.

So, what is the point here? The colors of the Rapture tally with the vision that Ezekiel had in 1:27, where the prophet, a younger contemporary of Jeremiah, saw Jesus like *"gleaming amber"* from *"his waist up"* in the NLT version of the Bible. Indeed, Jesus was *"flickering like a fire."*

When we read the NIV version of the Bible, the words are even more striking – for Christ looked like "*glowing metal, as if full of fire, and that from there down he looked like fire; and brilliant light surrounded him.*"The whitish yellow that I witnessed in the Rapture is described in Ezekiel 1:27 either as a *"burning flame, shining with splendor (NLT),"* or a *"brilliant light (NIV)."*

Between the translations, we can see that Christ is the Fire of God. Where else do we see this connection in the Bible? The Son of God has "*eyes like a flame of fire" or "flames of fire"* (Revelation 1:14, 2:18, 19:12 NIV), and who will be *"revealed from heaven in blazing fire with His powerful angels (2 Thessalonians 1:7 NIV)."* So, what I saw that night in my dream about the Rapture was the Fire of our Lord

God Jesus Christ. This is the symbolism and power of the Rapture – the Holy Spirit's Fire of our Lord God Jesus Christ.

It is important to note, that while films have sought to depict the Rapture in a flash of bright white light, it will instead be the amber-colored Fire of God that will take us on the day. Please note, it was beautiful, so peaceful and mesmerizing. And is that not what is written in verse 27? For the Lord Jesus Christ was *"shining with splendor."* Jesus is beautiful. Can I say that again? Jesus *is* beautiful. He *is.* He *is* beautiful. But what exactly is this beauty, what is this Fire of Jesus Christ the Redeemer?

We need to go to verse 28b to understand this better. *"This is what the glory of the LORD looked like to me. When I saw it, I fell face down on the ground…"*

The Fire of Jesus Christ is the glory of the Lord. This is the significance of the Rapture. Please note, this is not the function of the Rapture – we shall get to that later! Let's focus on the glory because all of this is about the glory of Him. For Jesus is the glory in the same way that He is the salvation, the judge, the way, the truth and the life. Once we understand that Jesus is the glory, we understand the purpose of the Rapture and here I reiterate the importance of this point.

The Rapture is for the glory of God the Son and completes His work on the Cross and finishes the Holy Spirit's work with the Church – for this is the will of God the Father.

In other words, the Rapture will glorify the Son and in turn will glorify the Father. The last time we saw this was the night before Christ went to the Cross:

"Father, the hour has come. Glorify your Son, that your Son may glorify you. [2] For you granted him authority over all people that he might give eternal life to all those you have given him. [3] Now this is eternal life: that they know you, the only true God, and Jesus Christ, whom you have sent. [4] I have brought you glory on earth by finishing the work you gave me to do. [5] And now, Father, glorify me in your presence with the glory I had with you before the world began (John 17:1-5 NIV)."

Is the significance of the Rapture starting to fill your soul yet? If not, that's okay, it will with time – not least on the day of the Rapture itself! Let's press on.

You see, on the day of the Rapture, the amber light that will appear on the walls, streets and hills will be the Fire of our Lord God Jesus Christ, it is the symbol of the Rapture, it is the marker. And its significance is that it is for the glory of the Son and in turn the glory of the Father.

We are to be all taken up personally by Jesus through the power of the Holy Spirit. For this is the will of the Father. I cannot stress the importance of this last point – *we are all to be taken up personally by Jesus*, who will have examined everyone's heart before the day of the Rapture and decided the fates of all His people. For Christ is the judge, and we will know the truth that day.

Again, I urge all to remain in a relationship with Christ because it is not enough to be baptized. You will see the importance of why at the end of this book when the Lord reveals what will happen to those who are left behind right after the Rapture. Keep the faith and stay in relationship brothers and sisters – this has never been more important than ever before!

Now, remember when I wrote that "for the second time, a bright strong orange light, an amber light, descended from the sky right in front of my eyes, it occupied all of my vision, it radiated all around me, surrounded me and as fast as it had come down, I felt a jolt as I was lifted up."

This is the moment when we can say or whisper as we are being taken up, "for your glory Jesus." For the moment we are lifted up, that moment that we feel that jolt like a train starting to move forward, that is the moment that our bodies are transformed and Jesus' work in us, His people on earth, is completed as we skyrocket to the heavens at unimaginable speed.

We can conclude at this point that the colors of the Rapture are the colors of the Fire of our Lord God Jesus Christ. Is this really new territory? No. Where else have we seen the Fire of God in relation to someone else being taken up to the heavens? Cue Elijah, who never died but was instead taken up to the sky in grand style.

"As they were walking along and talking together, suddenly a chariot of fire and horses of fire appeared and separated the two of them, and Elijah went up to heaven in a whirlwind (2 Kings 2:11 NIV)."

That all said, should we be afraid of this fire from our Sovereign God? Certainly not, at least for the Rapture, no. For our

Lord's fire has different natures, and it depends on the moment and how it is applied.

There is a great example in Numbers 11:1-3 NIV where the *"people complained about their hardships in the hearing of the Lord, and when he heard them his anger was aroused. Then fire from the Lord burned among them and consumed some of the outskirts of the camp. [2]When the people cried out to Moses, he prayed to the LORD and the fire died down. [3] So that place was called Taberah, because fire from the LORD had burned among them."*

We see another example of the Lord's fire and wrath in Leviticus 10:1-2 NIV: *"Aaron's sons Nadab and Abihu took their censers, put fire in them and added incense; and they offered unauthorized fire before the LORD, contrary to his command. [2] So fire came out from the presence of the LORD and consumed them, and they died before the LORD."* We also saw what happened with Sodom and Gomorrah!

It is important that we fear, revere, and deeply respect the Lord, loving and obeying Him. But is that not just Old Testament stuff? After all, Jesus went to the Cross, right? One might say that all we have to do now is just repent and our sins are forgiven, and hey, don't worry, everything is going to be okay. Nope, not quite.

Right now, the world is facing one environmental calamity after another. These are all expressions of the Lord's wrath towards society. Most people just think this is meteorology, climate change, global warming. Yes, that is one way of explaining it, but the Lord is deeply angered with what is happening to the world and it is going to get worse and worse as prophesied in Revelation. Here is just one example of what we can expect:

> *'[21] From the sky huge hailstones, each weighing about a hundred pounds, fell on people. And they cursed God on account of the plague of hail, because the plague was so terrible (Revelation 16:1 NIV)."*

For now, let's circle back to the topic of the Fire of God and how its amber color shows us how key moments in the Bible are connected to Christ. To stop the Israelites from complaining, the Lord God famously rained manna from heaven, indeed, it rained mercy from Jesus Christ. How do we know?

"Now manna was reminiscent of coriander seed, with an appearance similar to amber (Numbers 11:7 ISV)."

There we see that word amber in Numbers 11:7. Amber is a hallmark of Christ's ministry. It is the color of the Fire of God, the symbol of the Rapture. When we understand the symbolism of Ezekiel 1:26-28, 2 Kings 2:11, and Numbers 11:7, we know that Christ is behind all of these moments. It is little wonder that some of Christ's miracles included the feeding of the 4,000 (Mark 8:1-10), and the 5,000 (Matthew 14:13-21 NIV):

"Taking the five loaves and the two fish and looking up to heaven, he gave thanks and broke the loaves. Then he gave them to the disciples, and the disciples gave them to the people. [20] *They all ate and were satisfied, and the disciples picked up twelve basketfuls of broken pieces that were left over.* [21] *The number of those who ate was about five thousand men, besides women and children."*

We can see how the color amber and the manna from heaven in the Old Testament connects us intimately to Christ's feeding of the 5,000. These are all hallmarks of the Lord's ministry with His people, and one day in the future, we will see the color amber, or rather the Fire of God, leaving its mark on the Rapture. Color is an important but sometimes overlooked element of the Bible.

It is interesting to note that the word amber is mentioned some four times in the Old Testament (obs. there are many more references to the Fire of God). Amber is mentioned three times in Ezekiel (Ezekiel 1:4 KJV, 1:26 NLT, 8:2 KJV), and once in Numbers as we saw above. In Ezekiel 1:4, for example, we see that the fire in the sky is amber:

"And I looked, and, behold, a whirlwind came out of the north, a great cloud, and a fire infolding itself, and a brightness was about it, and out of the midst thereof as the colour of amber, out of the midst of the fire (Ezekiel 1:4 KJV)."

When we understand that amber is the color of the glory of our Lord Christ thanks to the prophet's revelation in Ezekiel

1:26-28, we see the Fire of God in a more personal light and can rest assured that the Rapture is going to be not only beautiful, glorious but also deeply personal for every one of us.

So, keep in mind the colors amber and bright whitish yellow for the day of the Rapture! For the fire of our living Lord God will whisk us away in a flash, lifting us up to meet Him in the sky. And if you are unsure as to what I mean by the color amber, the next time you are at the traffic lights, or behind a car indicating left or right, and you see that bright amber color, know that it will be very similar to the color of the Fire of God that you will see on the day of the Rapture.

It is interesting that the color amber is on traffic lights across the world and on the back of vehicles indicating direction! These things are never a coincidence and today, every time I see the color amber on a traffic light, I see it with a new relevance, I take the light in, I am in awe of it because it reminds me of Him every time, His glory and His immense love for all of us and the moment when He will come for us and lift us up to heaven.

Remember when I told of that moment of when I was enveloped in His loving and benign fire on all sides, that I was some 4 meters up in the air looking down at where I was standing – and then suddenly I saw myself as a blur? Cast your mind back to when I also mentioned that I felt a jolt and that that was when my body was *"transformed."*

Well, what transformed means that there was no sense of weight anymore, my body as I knew it was done. No more human or physical me. I was at that moment weightless and know that I will be completely weightless again in the future, heading up to the sky at an unfathomable speed in what felt pretty much like an instantaneous journey from where I was standing to my destination above.

I have replayed this moment so many times in my mind and the only words that still come to me are, *"for your glory Lord."* I can assure you that the moment of transformation and ascension is completely painless and impossible to explain. All I can say is that that moment was as real to me in that dream as it is now typing on the keyboard to you right now, writing in the Spirit and in the love of Christ.

Now, the closest I have ever felt to a moment like the one in the Rapture was when I was giving a service during the pandemic. I was more than 30 minutes into the service and had been praying for at least 10 minutes for the Holy Spirit to take over and step into my place.

Suddenly, I found myself looking at myself sitting at the chair talking to the folk via Teams. I was no longer in my body. I could not hear what I was saying, except that I could see myself talking to the folk online, sitting there in front of the screen as if nothing had happened. The Lord had stepped into my place as I had asked, He moved me out of my body and it was seamless.

This helped me understand what it felt to have an out-of-body experience, but more importantly I understood that this is how death feels like when the self is separated from the body. In a sense, it is like the Rapture as the feeling of separation is completely and utterly seamless and painless. Our bodies are the problem with all of their nerve receptors going off especially if they are in pain. We leave all of that behind with the Rapture – we leave and head to an eternity of peace in Christ.

But does this out-of-body experience seem so far-fetched? This is what it says in Mark 13:11 NIV:

"Whenever you are arrested and brought to trial, do not worry beforehand about what to say. Just say whatever is given you at the time, for it is not you speaking, but the Holy Spirit."

That Sunday service, I learned exactly what this verse meant, the Holy Spirit quite literally steps into your place and fully takes over. This sheds more light on the meaning of speaking in the Spirit, for I have learned by experience that the Lord often uses us to talk to others – many times I notice when I am being used to this effect and love it, but also that God the Spirit will step into our bodies and take over when requested. Have faith, trust the Lord and just believe!

So, let's recap here! The amber and gleaming yellow white lights will come in two stages (which I will later explain in greater detail the significance of the lights in terms of warning signs). The lights represent the Fire of God, which symbolizes the Rapture. This event is for the glory of the Son and that of the Father through the power of the Holy Spirit. The glory is the significance behind the Rapture. For Jesus is the glory in the same way that He is the salvation, the judge, the way, the truth and the life, for He is our Lord God. And the Son's glory glorifies the Father.

And lastly, the ascension will be painless, we will immediately experience weightlessness after the jolt as we are transformed, heading up to the sky at an unfathomable speed. We need not be afraid, it will not hurt. Are you ready for the greatest and fastest journey of your life?

Chapter 4
Where do we go? Origin and Destination

"Abraham was confidently looking forward to a city with eternal foundations, a city designed and built by God (Hebrews 11:10 NLT)."

When I started to understand the meaning behind the vision and figure out a number of key points such as who will be raptured, how it will happen, why it will happen, the warnings and calling from Lord Jesus Christ, the geography of it all still made little sense to me.

Here is the thing, the origin point of the Rapture for you and me will obviously be wherever you and I are on the planet at the moment of the Rapture. We will be raptured because we are in relationship with Christ. Simple.

So, you will be raptured wherever you are but what about the destination? In the vision, I went up to the sky but where? I knew that I was not in heaven in the sense that I understand heaven to be. I was in an enclosed space, with no windows, no views and yet light reflected off the precious stones on the walls that could have been made of Beryl or possibly Noreena Jasper. The walls were a greyish white. Another thing that I had noticed was that while I could not see what I was wearing, I was no longer holding my iPhone.

While I clearly did not know where I was, my iPhone did not get transformed with me, nor should it. My iPhone is somewhere on the floor of that office in that church for someone to try to hack or just leave there, or throw away, and I am grateful that the Lord God gave me this important detail.

You see when we arrive up there, we will no longer have watches on us, our clothes will no longer be what we bought at Zara, Gucci, C&A or Primark, our oldest and favorite jewelry no more, zip, nada, diddly squat, and certainly no smartphone. Nope, we will have something else, and whatever it is, it will be extremely tasteful because our Lord God takes care of all of the details and wastes nothing.

We should not worry. Did our Lord God not clothe Adam and Eve with tunics in Genesis 3:21 after they ate the forbidden fruit of knowledge? Did not the Lord sacrifice one or two animals to make those tunics so that Adam and Eve were covered with His justice to (temporarily) atone for their sins?

And in sacrificing the animals for the payment of Adam and Eve's disobedience, did our Lord, who demands justice for sins that are committed, not announce the need for the perfect sacrifice (Lamb) to go to the Cross and pay for the sins of the world (on a permanent basis) and settle an impossible debt that we could never redeem ourselves by dying in our place on the Cross and suffering the cruelest of deaths? Was not Christ's sacrifice consequently prophesied in Eden (Genesis 3:15, 3:21)?

Yes, He did all that in Eden, amen? Amen! So imagine, just how much He will take care of us once we are up there with Him! We should not worry, we have so much to look forward to, for the Lord provides.

So instead of iPhones, watches, wedding rings and other items on our body, we will receive crowns, an inheritance and a white stone with a new name, symbolizing our innocence and announcing our right to be there with our Lord God (Micah 7:18, Isaiah 58:13-14, Ephesians 1:10-11, 13-14, 18, Colossians 3:23-24, Hebrews 9:15, 11:8, Revelation 2:17). But that takes us back to that question, where was I in the sky? In 1 Thessalonians 4:17, it states that we will go to "*meet the Lord in the air. And so we will be with the Lord forever.*"

Here is the thing, I did not meet Jesus Christ once I was up there, though I was up there for just seconds – just enough time to notice my surroundings before the vision itself ended. I believe that the point of the vision was not to see Christ but to witness the Rapture, report back to humanity and warn others about the need to be prepared for the last day.

Plus, the verse in 1 Thessalonians 4:17 states *"to meet the Lord in the air."* It does not mean that we will all immediately meet the Lord in the air once we are raptured. This is a widely held misconception. The words *"to meet"* in the 17th verse simply imply that this is something that will happen between Christ and His believers in the future.

To meet does not communicate immediacy in itself. We also have to appreciate that the Rapture is no small undertaking. Billions of Christians and children are being taken up at the same time worldwide. Can you imagine that kind of logistics and undertaking? To move billions of people across the globe would be impossible for us but the Lord need only command it by His authority for it to happen.

So, take heart, for we will meet the Lord once we are taken up there, and we will be with Him forever. Plus, and this is important to note, had I seen Jesus during the vision, the emphasis, weighting and interpretation of the vision would have clearly changed.

Instead, the Lord wants us to focus on being prepared for the Rapture by calling all of us into a relationship ahead of the Rapture (more to come on this and why baptized unchurched Christians need to change their posture soonest). We would all do well to heed the warnings presented by the Holy Spirit in the vision (more to come on this later), for the Lord wants us to prepare. Did not Noah get a 120-year head start on building the ark before the great flood? This book acts as a similar heads-up just in a different format.

Now, returning to the issue of destination and where I found myself in the sky. Remember I had written that it was in an enclosed yet very beautiful palatial place with precious stones gleaming in the walls? Well, I sensed that the same Brazilian family that was with me in the church study that day, was also up there with me. The Lord allowed me to sense them but not see them clearly – they remained out of focus or rather blurred more than anything else (I did try to discern them but was not allowed to).

Why would I not be able to discern them? Well, there is a lot of wisdom in this and as I delve into the ramifications of the Brazilian family, which was not my own, I kind of feel that if I try to figure all of this out I am going to find myself in a quasi-Back-To-The-Future moment. How so?

First, if I already know the family that I will be raptured with on that last day in a church in England somewhere, I am pretty sure I would end up second-guessing my movements right up to the day of the Rapture.

If that happens, then, I will have succumbed to some kind of obsession and that would not be healthy. What I do know is that I have not yet met this family but I will obviously meet them in the future, and I must be content with that for I do not want to live a life of second-guessing my next steps or myself.

A life of second-guessing and doubt is not how the Lord wants us to live. When we listen to our doubts, we are listening to the enemy and not what Christ wants for us!

So, enough speculation and let's go back to that moment in the sky and destination, and bear with me as I eliminate certain factors and move us closer to the answer of destination. You see, I knew that I did not end up in heaven but didn't know why and I am not sure why I was so blinded to the obviousness of where I was.

I was caught up with the notion that I was in some palatial room somewhere and kept asking myself where could that possibly be? There is no Google Maps for this kind of thing and I would never have dared to think that I of all people had seen a glimpse, albeit brief, of the Kingdom of God!

For nearly two months I was at a loss as to where I had ended up in the sky until I met Pastor Robson, who was visiting our church. I told him about my vision, I wanted to see his reaction and what he thought because I knew he was a man filled with the Holy Spirit and walks with the Lord.

I put my vision to the test and told Robson about what had happened that June night and the Lord's revelation in my dream. As I was finishing and told him about where I ended up, I timidly confessed that I didn't yet know what it meant. He smiled back.

This is what he said to me: "I really felt that, the Holy Spirit spoke to me as you told me about the vision, it is true, and where you ended up is easy, the place where you went to is Zion, just go to Hebrews 11:10, it is *the city* in the sky. Others have told me about being taken to Zion."

One of the key parts of the vision just slotted into place. I was astonished and I never use that word to describe any of my emotions, like ever. As soon as I had finished talking to Pastor Robson, I looked up the verse in Hebrews and this is what it said:

"Abraham was confidently looking forward to a city with eternal foundations, a city designed and built by God (Hebrews 11:10 NLT)."

Questions raced through my mind. What could Abraham possibly have anything to do with the Rapture? What about this city? Is this the same city at the end of Revelation? Is this the centerpiece of the Kingdom of God? Have I seen the Kingdom of God? Me? Why me?

As soon as I asked such questions, I remembered how I had been intermittently praying at bedtime to see something of heaven. And the Lord had answered my prayer! He never fails! I had not just been given a vision, I had received a glimpse of where every man, woman and child in our Lord God will end up for all eternity when we will live in the presence of our Adonai Elohim.

I had witnessed a very small part of everlasting to everlasting in the Father and in the Lamb. I had gone to that place where we will all bask in His light, His love, His wisdom, His peace, His righteousness, and joy forever, and by this place I mean the Kingdom of God. I had been to the Kingdom of God albeit ever so briefly. I had been afforded an incredible opportunity to see that one room, a moment that is most treasured and indelible in my mind. It was like a dream coming true for me.

Ever since studying at seminary, I had been fascinated with the Kingdom of God – where we will all be royalty, immortal and the Lord's treasured possession. We will be a kingdom of priests in a place where there is no disease, no disappointment, no depression, no delusion, no dismay, no demonic oppression.

In short, Pastor Robson's words and their revelation left me giddy like a schoolchild. Really. As I quietly reveled in the realization that I had been to the Kingdom of God – the centerpiece of Christ's ministry and preaching focus, I revisited Revelation 21 to soak in John's vision of the magnificent and truly awesome place. This is what John, Apostle of our Lord God Jesus Christ of Nazareth, witnessed in a vision during his exile on the island of Patmos:

"I saw the Holy City, the new Jerusalem, coming down out of heaven from God, prepared as a bride beautifully dressed for her husband. [3]

And I heard a loud voice from the throne saying, "Look! God's dwelling place is now among the people, and he will dwell with them. They will be his people, and God himself will be with them and be their God. [4] *'He will wipe every tear from their eyes. There will be no more death' or mourning or crying or pain, for the old order of things has passed away…* [18] *The wall was made of jasper, and the city of pure gold, as pure as glass.* [19] *The foundations of the city walls were decorated with every kind of precious stone. The first foundation was jasper, the second sapphire, the third agate, the fourth emerald,* [20] *the fifth onyx, the sixth ruby, the seventh chrysolite, the eighth beryl, the ninth topaz, the tenth turquoise, the eleventh jacinth, and the twelfth amethyst.*[f] [21] *The twelve gates were twelve pearls, each gate made of a single pearl. The great street of the city was of gold, as pure as transparent glass (Revelation 21:2-4, 18-21, NIV)."*

I think the verses are pretty self-explanatory and revealing of the beauty of the Kingdom of God but just to make it very clear – we are going to Zion, or New Jerusalem, and don't ask me how everybody is going to fit up there because billions are going up – this includes the resurrected dead and the transformed living (1 Thessalonians 4:16-17).

What a glorious day the Rapture will be! Indeed, as I wrote about this, the Holy Spirit brought to mind an important verse to add here from Revelation 7:9 NIV:

"After this I looked, and there before me was a great multitude that no one could count, from every nation, tribe, people and language, standing before the throne and before the Lamb. They were wearing white robes and were holding palm branches in their hands."

Are you excited? As each day passes, the arrival of the Rapture grows in my heart, I cannot wait! One day more means one day less on earth. And if this has not yet become clear, yes, we are going to New Jerusalem, and yes we are eternal, we will not die, we will live forever (or never-ending time) with our heavenly Father and the Lamb (Revelation 21).

Your mind, your essence, the "you" that is your consciousness, your memories and experiences, who you were, remain intact once you are up there. I would like to repeat this, we do not die, our memories are not wiped out, we are eternal in Christ.

We will not be like those who spend eternity burning in a lake of fire and foul-smelling sulfur, being made to remember and think on their sins, regretting the decisions they made, the things they did, the iniquity they loved and above all – turning down Christ's love in their lives and rejecting Him.

Now, let's return to Abraham and ask the following question: What does Abraham have to do with all of this and why is he so relevant to the Rapture and the Kingdom of God?

To answer this question, we need to return to Genesis and the time of Abraham. However, it is important to note that every time a subject is mentioned for the first time in Genesis, we need to bear in mind that this first reference becomes the standard by which we should interpret such an issue anywhere else in the Bible.

For example, the definition of sin is in Genesis 2 and 3. This includes its treatment, punishment, impact, cost, condemnation, justice, and atonement. Whenever we read about sin and its implications in the New Testament, we can always go back to Genesis 2 and 3 to understand the origins of iniquity.

Another key term that appears in Genesis, is covenant, which is an accord that comes with a series of conditions as well as blessings and promises from the Lord. It is a critically important word in Genesis, especially for all of those who are part of the Lord's people to this day.

So how did the covenant evolve between God and man? Well, the Lord first made a covenant with Adam, making mankind in the image of God, fruitful, and giving us dominion over the earth and animals (Genesis 1:27-28). The second covenant was with Noah.

The Lord promised that He would not flood the planet again, and blessed Noah's sons so that they would be fruitful, increase in number and fill the earth:

"I establish my covenant with you: Never again will all life be destroyed by the waters of a flood; never again will there be a flood to destroy the earth (Genesis 9:11 NIV)."

The next covenant was with Abraham – and we can see how this covenant is more elaborate, more specific and filled with more blessings than the previous two covenants with Adam and Noah.

However, such covenants come with conditions and tests from the Lord. For Abraham, this was no different and we reach a critical point in Genesis 22 where the Lord tested the covenant that was established between them. For those unfamiliar with Abraham's life at this point, the Lord had asked the prophet to take his only son, whom he loved, and sacrifice him as a "*burnt offering on a mountain (Genesis 22:2 NIV).*"

Abraham was 100 years old when Isaac was born and was a gift from the Lord (Genesis 18:10). The Lord promised Abraham he would have a child even in his old age. This promise was made before Abraham appealed to the Lord to stop Him from destroying Sodom and Gomorrah. The prophet saw the destruction and the consequence of disobeying the Lord. It would have had a profound effect on Him.

Consequently, when the Lord asked Abraham to sacrifice his firstborn, his one and only son, the prophet was prepared to do just that. Abraham had to obey not just because he feared the Lord and had seen the destruction of Sodom and Gomorrah but also because he had established a covenant with God. What does that mean?

Well, typically, such an accord involves an exchange of robes, belts, weapons, enemies, names and most profound of all, the exchange of firstborn sons. Abraham had to go through with the sacrifice. He had made a covenant with Adonai Elohim and just as he was about to sacrifice his one and only son on the mountain, the Lord intervened, stopped him, and provided a ram instead.

This is how our Lord responded to Abraham's faithfulness:

"I swear by myself, declares the Lord that because you have done this and have not withheld your son, your only son, [17] I will surely bless you and make your descendants as numerous as the stars in the sky and as the sand on the seashore. Your descendants will take possession of the cities of their enemies, [18] and through your offspring all nations on earth will be blessed, because you have obeyed me (Genesis 22:16-18 NIV)."

The Lord not only stopped Abraham from sacrificing his only and one son but He also promised to honor the same covenant with the prophet's descendants. This is highlighted in verse 22, *"through your offspring all nations on earth will be blessed, because you have obeyed me."*

You see, what happened in Genesis 22, was a precursor to what would happen on the Cross when the Lord would give His one and only Son to save the world, and by doing so, He honored His covenant with Abraham and His people: *"For God so loved the world that he gave his one and only Son, that whoever believes in him shall not perish but have eternal life (John 3:16 NIV)."*

Simply put, we are all blessed through Jesus Christ – a direct descendant of Abraham (42 generations apart). Gentiles get to enjoy the blessings that the Lord promised to Abraham when we confess our sins and accept Jesus into our hearts. We are heirs to the covenant between Abraham and the Lord. The blessings are also passed onto us!

So now that we understand this covenantal connection, we can now return to the theme of the Kingdom of God within the context of Abraham. Let's look at Hebrews 11:

"[8] It was by faith that Abraham obeyed when God called him to leave home and go to another land that God would give him as his inheritance. He went without knowing where he was going. [9] And even when he reached the land God promised him, he lived there by faith—for he was like a foreigner, living in tents. And so did Isaac and Jacob, who inherited the same promise. [10] Abraham was confidently looking forward to a city with eternal foundations, a city designed and built by God (Hebrews 11:8-10 NLT)."

So, what is the connection? Allow me to rewrite Hebrews 11:8, 10, so it becomes a little clearer as to how our Christian life can be a pilgrimage just like that of Abraham's.

"It is by faith that all of us come to Jesus and obey our Lord God, it is by faith that we leave what we think to be our permanent home and head to the promised land up in the sky where our Lord God will give us our inheritance. We go without knowing exactly where we are going… but like Abraham we are confidently looking forward to the city of God, the city with eternal foundations, New Jerusalem, Zion, the city in the sky that God himself designed and built for all eternity for His people."

For this is where Adonai Elohim wants to take us, by accepting Christ as our savior and making Him Lord over our lives, we become part of Adonai Elohim's people, and because of this, we will eventually make our way to our permanent home, the Kingdom of God and know the presence of our Lord God for all eternity.

For we the Gentiles "constitute the extended people of the Abraham covenant, to be the agent of God's blessing to the nations in the name and for the glory of the Lord Jesus Christ (Christopher Wright, Mission of God p.67 Kindle edition)." And this is how Abraham's descendants become as "*numerous as the stars (Genesis 22:17),*" and why we see a future countless multitude standing before the Lamb (Revelation 7:9-10). The mission of bringing people to Christ has never been more important!

So, Abraham is important not just to us in terms of living righteously by faith, depending on the Lord, sharing in and enjoying his covenantal blessings, but also helping us know where every Christian will end up on the day of the Rapture. His longing for the city of God with eternal foundations points to our final destination – points to our permanent home, points to where we will go and end up being reconciled with our Adonai Elohim for all time. This is the point.

Abraham not only saw the blessings that are coming to us (his people, the people of God, Jews and Gentiles) but also where we will end up together in the sky forever. Abraham matters. He has already seen the pilgrimage that we are taking and blazed a trail for all of us. So yes, Abraham matters for so many reasons. His journey is ours for we are a part of his people. He is also our patriarch whether we understand that or not.

For we will all one day be standing before the throne, holding palm branches and crying out in a loud voice, "*Salvation belongs to our God, who sits on the throne and to the Lamb (Revelation 7:9 NIV).*"

So, like Abraham, the Father of Many Nations and the Father of the people of God, we too should long for that same city in the sky with eternal foundations that is "designed and built by God."

And like Abraham, we must remember that we too are living in temporary homes (versus his living in tents), moving from one place to another, changing addresses, cities, states or countries, before we go to our permanent and final resting place - the Kingdom of God, which is represented by the holy city with eternal foundations, or New Jerusalem.

The Kingdom of God is not to be taken lightly, it is not just an incredibly beautiful place that we can look forward to in the future where we will live with God the Father and God the Son in New Jerusalem. It is not just about the future reign of our Lord God, it is all about doing the will of the Father. When Jesus taught us to pray, He said our Father's Kingdom comes when His will is done earth as it is in heaven.

What Jesus is saying is that the future blessings of an eternal life in the Kingdom of God without disease, stress, financial worries or persecution, can be enjoyed today in the present. How so? By doing the will of the Father, we bring the future blessings of the Kingdom of God into the present. Bear with me on this, it all sounds a little too fantastic to grasp, but people are cured in Christ and freed from demonic oppression in Christ every day because someone obeyed the will of the Father and prayed for someone else.

Let me give you an example of how the Kingdom of God works. I visited a man and prayed for the restoration of his health, his pastorship and his marriage just a week earlier before writing this text. He had had a stroke three weeks before that in late 2023. His right side (arm and hand) was paralyzed.

The doctors did not know how long it would take for him to recover feeling or movement in his right side. After two hours of prayer, sensation had returned to his arm, then it gradually returned to his hand followed by feeling in finger after finger. Following four hours of healing and prophetic prayer, I had lifted his arm and asked him to move his hand.

Nothing at that point but the Lord showed me in my mind the man's right hand, holding a pen and writing. His daughter informed me that her father used his right hand to write his sermons, using a pen. I was encouraged, however, the time had come to leave.

I assured her that her father would fully recover (but didn't mention that I had already seen him fully recovered in the future, standing in a dapper suit, smiling and being covered in confetti at his daughter's future wedding that she does not yet know about because she has not yet been proposed to).

Shortly after I had left, I received news that he was able to move his arm and right hand again and was on his way to recovery. The Lord is good, and the future blessing of the Kingdom of God was revealed in that pastor's life that day to the glory of our Lord God!

This is a recent example of the future Kingdom of God in action in the present! The future blessings of the Kingdom of God are brought into the present. And this is not fiction! The miracles that marked Christ's ministry continue to this day because the Lord gave us the use of His mighty and powerful name.

Every Christian can use His name to contribute to the Kingdom of God by telling others about Jesus, by loving, serving and helping them as well as revealing the will of the Father. All of us are called to seek and appropriate the Kingdom of God today by accepting Christ and following the way of life that Jesus gave us.

To help us understand this better, Jesus preached, lived and practiced the Kingdom of God during His ministry on earth. Christ preached the Good News of the Kingdom of God wherever he went including the streets and the synagogues. He talked about the kingdom through parables and practiced the Kingdom of God in his ministry by healing and delivering people from demons.

Ideally, every Pastor, minister and priest should proclaim the Kingdom of God at every service – for this is what Jesus did and this is why Jesus went to the Cross – to establish a bridge between us and God the Father so that we can be reconciled with Him and go to our permanent home - the Kingdom of God.

For we are to be reconciled with the Father after Adam and Eve disobeyed Him in Eden and separated us from our Lord God. Now, in 2024, the Kingdom of God is a promise that we carry in our hearts, a promise that we must share with others.

For we arrive at the kingdom by faith, by accepting Jesus in our hearts.

To understand the focus of Jesus' ministry better, the Gospel of Mark is an excellent example and roadmap to the Kingdom of God. Jesus gives us a glimpse of the Kingdom of God by healing folk, raising the dead and casting our evil spirits, for in the Kingdom of God there will be no illness, crying, pain, grief or mourning (Revelation 21:4).

Importantly, there will also be no more Satan and his hoard, which relentlessly seeks to corrupt our minds, break our hearts and destroy our souls and lives. Oh joy, I can tell you that now!

Thanks to Jesus, you and I can benefit from the promise and blessings of the Kingdom of God in the present time right now if we believe in the name of Jesus Christ of Nazareth (John 1:12, 1 John 5:13, John 3:18, Matthew 12:21). We too can heal others (Acts 3:16) or free others from spirits (Acts 16:18) and much more, for Jesus said:

"[13] And I will do whatever you ask in my name, so that the Father may be glorified in the Son. [14] You may ask me for anything in my name, and I will do it (John 14:13-14 NIV)."

For many, however, they will remain skeptical and say, "that's nice, but I am not Jesus and nor am I an apostle, miracles are only in the Bible and really do not exist." I say, and there are many like me who not only agree but also know, "nope, that is wrong."

Be encouraged, keep seeking the Lord and growing closer and closer to Him - for the key to the Kingdom of God is not only accepting Jesus, living in relationship with Him but learning to hear the will of the Father and obeying the Lord in His commands. Allow me another example before we return to the ins and outs of the Rapture!

One day in late October, 2023, the Lord told me to pray for a man, who could barely walk, his left leg was completely crooked. To understand his problem better in words, it would be like walking on a metal stilt that had buckled under pressure and was bent right in the middle. His left leg was shaped like a V tilted to the side. It must have been very painful for him to walk. I went up to him and asked him if I could pray.

Okay, that is an oversimplification of what happened, let's take a step back and allow me to take you into the moment. I was on a fairly busy city street in Osasco just outside a store. The spring morning was sweltering, and I was in a hurry because I had a flight to Mexico the next day. I had a suit to find for a blessing at a wedding and I had not found what I wanted at the city's center.

On the way back to the car park, I stopped as my wife went into a shop. As I stood there, I noticed there were five-odd people around me on the pavement. There was a lot of noise from the traffic and folk talking around me. Suddenly, I heard a voice that made me turn round. The man, who was speaking, spoke in a muffled fashion that I could not understand.

He was talking to two others, who worked at the shop, and I had no idea what he said, I simply could not fathom him. However, the other two seemed to know what he had uttered and responded in kind. At that moment, I received a command from the Lord to pray for the man with the muffled voice. I looked at him as he talked to others before he crossed the road with much difficulty and limped into a car park.

My internal spiritual radar was switched on – the Lord wanted me to go after the lame man and ask a stranger if I could pray for him. I felt like a stalker in every sense, and while for a split second I was reluctant to go across the road after a man in a car park, I knew better than to discuss with the Lord whether I should go or not.

Such arguments with Him are utterly pointless. They always feel like a tug of war between my mind, emotions and will (my soul) and the Lord's will. Back then, I found myself resisting His will because of apathy, lack of time, embarrassment, or an underlying feeling that it was all just a little too inconvenient.

However, this is not what Jesus asks of us and while this whole conversation went on in my head for a matter of a few seconds, I knew that I had to obey because my ministry is in the streets, I had been called to pray for those wherever I go.

Moreover, I had asked the Lord just a few weeks earlier what would be required from me to live in fellowship in the Holy Spirit. God the Spirit replied with one word – obedience. That is the price for such intimate fellowship.

When you have a path to walk with the Lord, you must walk it in obedience. So that point in my mind ended that extremely brief one-sided argument that really got me nowhere, and I crossed the road, sheepishly following the lame man who had gone into the car park.

I found him by the booth and throwing all caution to the wind, I went up to him and said, "can I pray for you?" He replied yes. I was glad. I then asked, "do you know Jesus?" He said yes. "Do you love Jesus?" Again, he said yes.

"Do you mind if I lay my hands on you as I pray? Again, the response was yes. I felt relieved as I placed my right hand on the stranger's chest and my left on his back, and we started to pray. I started to pray in tongues and asked the man to confess his sins to the Lord. The Holy Spirit led the prayer and flowed into his chest with His energy and peace.

As we prayed, I asked the Lord to restore his speech, thinking that this is what mattered to the man most. However, after a few minutes or so of prayer, I felt pins and needles in my right leg. I wondered if the Holy Spirit was giving me some kind of direction or hint as to what was happening to the man, so I asked him if he felt something in his leg and when I opened my eyes, he was beaming at me.

"Yes!!!" He was flexing his left leg, it was straight. "My left knee, my left knee," he said. I concluded the prayer shortly afterward and gave thanks to the Lord as I looked at the man I had never met until a few minutes earlier. Overjoyed, we hugged.

The man, who worked in a car park (where we were at that moment), walked fast to a car at the entrance, beaming while stretching his left leg as if it were brand new, just off the shelf. "I have to return to work," he said smiling, looking back before disappearing behind a car.

I looked on and contemplated that moment. I was in awe of the Lord. "God loves that man," I exclaimed to the car park cashier who was trying to understand what had just happened. What a week, I thought. Just two days earlier, I was praying for a baptized unbeliever when the Holy Spirit expelled four demons out of him and anointed him with laughter (he walked away laughing and could not stop.)

So, what does this all mean? The Gospel of the Kingdom of God is alive and well today. Many more miracles happened that week – many prophecies, a blessing at a wedding, and lots of messages of love and encouragement from the Lord to His people.

The Kingdom of God is here so long as we do the Father's will. Knowing the Lord, knowing His will and being obedient are key if you serve or want to serve and want to deliver the Gospel with His power. That is just a glimpse of the future blessings of the Kingdom of God today in our day-to-day lives, and it is for such examples – that are happening across the world today – that we should look to the future promise of the Kingdom of God with hope and confidence in Jesus Christ – for He is our way to salvation, our way to the Father, our way to the everlasting in His presence.

For without Jesus, salvation is impossible, without Jesus' sacrifice in our place, our sins cannot be paid and only with Jesus *via the Holy Spirit* can we confidently come before God the Father's throne in prayer (Hebrews 4:16). In short, without Jesus, reconciliation of our sinful bodies to the Heavenly Father is impossible. Until we are all there together in New Jerusalem on that glorious day, we have the promises in the Bible to inspire us and keep motivating us to keep seeking the Lord and get closer to Him. We have the miracles in the Gospels and glimpses of the Kingdom of God itself – principally in Revelation 21-22 - to drive us deeper into our relationship with Jesus. And this is a personal favourite of mine in Hebrews – what a spectacle – can you wait for this day?

"22 But you have come to Mount Zion, to the city of the living God, the heavenly Jerusalem. You have come to thousands upon thousands of angels in joyful assembly, 23 to the church of the firstborn, whose names are written in heaven. You have come to God, the Judge of all, to the spirits of the righteous made perfect, 24 to Jesus the mediator of a new covenant, and to the sprinkled blood that speaks a better word than the blood of Abel (Hebrews 12:22-24)."*

(*NB firstborn has multiple meanings from the covenantal promise to Jesus being the first from among the dead to resurrect and go to heaven, paving the way for the dead and the living to do the same ahead of the Rapture – see Colossians 1:15-18 and 1 Thessalonians 4:16. Firstborn, also in Hebrews 1:6, does not mean that Christ was created by God.)

Ultimately, what is clear is that on the day of the Rapture itself, it is really not so important where we finish our lives on earth but where we will end up, will it be upstairs or downstairs for you? With Jesus or without Jesus? Or are you yet to ask the most important question in your life for your eternity depends on that answer – do I accept Jesus Christ as my Savior and Lord?

Indeed, geography matters – will you be taken up or will you die and be consumed in God's fire of wrath? Either we bask in His fury or love for all eternity. Now, if that all sounds Old Testament to you – hell is exactly that.

Remember the story of the rich man and a beggar named Lazarus in Luke 16:19-31 NIV, where the rich man ends up in hell and he sees Lazarus with Abraham "far away" across a "great chasm" and says,

"[24]Father Abraham, have pity on me and send Lazarus to dip the tip of his finger in water and cool my tongue, because I am in agony in this fire.' [25] *But Abraham replied, 'Son, remember that in your lifetime you received your good things, while Lazarus received bad things, but now he is comforted here and you are in agony.* [26] *And besides all this, between us and you a great chasm has been set in place, so that those who want to go from here to you cannot, nor can anyone cross over from there to us."*

There is no way out, no way back from hell and no salvation in this lifetime without Jesus. So, where you finish the race is infinitely more important than where you are when the Rapture happens, but it is important that we are all in contact with our loved ones at that last moment, that last minute before we are taken up, that they, like you, are prepared for the Rapture.

That will matter greatly, for families across the world will be separated that day. Many in Christ will be taken up but many will also sadly stay behind. That number will sadly be in the many tens of millions (if not hundreds of millions).

So, let's quickly recap! Billions will disappear on the day of the Rapture, and those who are taken up will include approximately one billion children. The event will be marked by amber and gleaming yellow white lights that will appear across the planet in two stages.

These lights represent the Fire of Jesus Christ, our Lord God. The fire symbolizes the Rapture, which will reveal the glory of the Son and the Father through the power of the Holy Spirit. It is this glory that is the significance behind the Rapture.

On top of this, we will all be transformed in an instant and taken up at unimaginable speed to the Kingdom of God, our permanent home, otherwise known as New Jerusalem. There we will be reunited with loved ones. It will be beautiful. For it is the city in the sky with eternal foundations that Abraham yearned for in his heart!

For we are the extended part of his people when we confess Jesus Christ as our Savior and Lord. And when we do this, we too can enjoy the blessings and promises of the Abrahamic covenant made new by the blood of Christ.

So, where we are on earth when we are raptured is not as important as where we end up. However, it does matter who we are with just before the Rapture happens. This issue becomes even more acute if we are the ones who are in a relationship with Christ but find ourselves around people who are baptized but are not in a relationship with the Lord. Just imagine that moment! Someone somewhere is certainly going to face that difficulty!

Perhaps, the Lord will put you in that very situation so as to urge others to confess their sins and ask for forgiveness. We will have to be quick on our toes. There will be very little time (will reveal more on this later).

However, this is not a recipe for success if you are a Christian who does not go to church and thinks it is okay all the same and that salvation is guaranteed because you are baptized. I reiterate this because it is so important, we must be in a relationship with the Lord no matter what! We cannot afford to be left behind. Why? What could be so terrible? The tribulation? The antichrist? Well, this takes us next to the warnings. What must we know about this last day?

What should we tell others, for if you are reading this text, I urge you in the name of Jesus, to warn them – Revival is coming, it will be unmistakable and impossible to miss, but so many baptized Christians are going to be left behind after the Rapture and the consequences of that will be terrible, unthinkable.

Chapter 5
The warnings and timing of the Rapture

"[51]But let me reveal to you a wonderful secret. We will "not all die, but we will all be transformed! [52] It will happen in a moment, in the blink of an eye, when the last trumpet is blown. For when the trumpet sounds, those who have died will be raised to live forever. And we who are living will also be transformed (1 Corinthians 15:51-52 NLT)."

The Good News is that the Kingdom of God and eternal life in Christ are so very near, and the "*wonderful secret*" is that most of us, who are alive today, will still be alive by the time of the Rapture. Brothers and sisters in Christ – so many of us will not know death. Amen?

Indeed, the end will come sooner than so many think but not so soon as a number believe (churches are already warning that it will be in 2024, nope, it will not, the Lord is building up toward Revival first and then the Rapture). So many Christians, who are truly in Christ today, will not know death and will instead know what it is to be taken up in the Rapture – a moment that is marked by a jolt before corporal transformation – an almost instantaneous ascension into the sky.

However, and as before, the revelation of the Rapture comes with a number of warnings, none least being that the antichrist is already among us. It does not take much to figure this out – circles of the world's elite are already looking at ways for a one world government. So much so that billionaire Elon Musk warned about the risks of a "single world government" and how it could lead to the end of civilization during the World Government Summit in 2023.

The creation of such a government creates the ideal conditions for the antichrist, which will have 42 months of rule, subjecting all nations worldwide (Revelation 13:5). On top of this, society is unwittingly or unknowingly being brainwashed into worshipping the devil typically through mainstream media, namely music, streaming series, shows, films, online portals, magazines and newspapers. Sin is in fashion, everything goes and the lines between good and evil are blurred to the point that evil is good and good is evil, making it all the more challenging for the Lord's people in the last days.

Now, before we tackle the antichrist in a separate chapter, let's look at what is more important, the warnings of the Rapture itself. Our Lord God in His wisdom provides us with three distinct warnings and only through nearly two months of meditation on the dream, talking to pastors, pouring over verses in the Bible and being guided by the Holy Spirit was I able to comprehend the context of the warnings by understanding the context of the timing of the Rapture itself.

Just to clarify, I am not trying to say when the Rapture will happen, instead, I am focused on what the vision showed me about the Rapture itself. You see there is a big gaping question when it comes to timing. Let's compare. Firstly, it is believed that Noah took a century to 120 years to build the ark.

For Lot, the warning that Sodom and Gomorrah would be destroyed came the night before (Genesis 19:1-14). So how much time can we expect when we receive the warning that the Rapture is about to happen? Before I clarify this point, it is important to highlight that it took some two months to understand the period of time between my talking to my father, the appearing of the amber and whitish-yellow gleaming lights and the moment that I was taken up to the sky.

At first, I thought I had probably witnessed the last 30 minutes of my life when I first tried to understand the dream. It at least felt that way in the vision as I talked to my father on the phone. However, time in dreams is never the same as time in the real world. Time with our Lord is also the same, in the sense, that time rushes by as we immerse ourselves in prayer. When we spend time with Christ, what may feel like a moment could easily be two hours.

So how long do we really have on the day of the Rapture? To be fair, I had no idea. I kept going over the dream and nada. Simply nada, blip, zero. I was none the wiser. That was when the

Holy Spirit came to the rescue (yet again and not for the last time either) and guided me to the following verse:

"[51]But let me reveal to you a wonderful secret. We will "not all die, but we will all be transformed! [52] It will happen in a moment, in the blink of an eye, when the last trumpet is blown. For when the trumpet sounds, those who have died will be raised to live forever. And we who are living will also be transformed (1 Corinthians 15:51-52 NLT)."

Paul the Apostle, who wrote about the Rapture in his letters to the early churches, witnessed the final moment of the Church on earth in either a dream or a vision. He saw the living and the dead raptured on the final day. Paul is one of many sleeping in Christ and his body will be resurrected soon enough (alongside other famous Christians including Shakespeare, Isaac Newton, Charles Dickens, C.S. Lewis, Mother Theresa, Charles Spurgeon, Queen Elizabeth II and so many more – what a glorious day it will be for all in Christ from the least to the greatest in Him).

Now, why is this all important? Well, Paul, who was the greatest apostle of them all and commissioned by Christ on his way to Damascus (Acts 9:3-5), witnessed the Rapture in such a way that he left a key time stamp in 1 Corinthians 15:52.

"*It will happen in a moment, in the blink of an eye, when the last trumpet is blown.*" Before we look at the importance of the "*blink of an eye,*" we need to note that Paul hears the last trumpet, I did not.

In fact, I heard nothing throughout the whole dream except for my own voice when I was talking to my father. The Heavenly Father did not want me to recognize any sounds or more importantly voices! There is great wisdom in this.

After all, here I am breaking down the vision, detail by detail – can you imagine what I would have written had I heard the Trumpet blaring? Now let's move to the second point and the time marker. Paul wrote that it will happen in a "moment," or more specifically in the "blink of an eye" in 1 Corinthians 15:51-52.

A moment can be anything really, it can mean a minute or 10 minutes, who is to say, however, Paul wrote in "the blink of an eye." It takes just 100 to 150 milliseconds to blink. This is twice the speed of the reaction time of a Formula 1 driver, who typically reacts at 200 to 300 milliseconds. In short and cutting to the chase, the Rapture is going to be fast and with hindsight it allows me to understand the timing of the vision that I saw that June night.

Initially, I thought I had witnessed the last 30 minutes of my life after I had seen the dream. By the time I had been able to digest the time marker left by Paul, I realized that I had only seen the last minute of my life on earth before the Rapture.

So, here is the first warning, the Rapture is going to be fast and there is going to be little time in terms of a heads-up. You will have a minute to repent but what about the others who are not in a relationship? And here is another problem - the "blink of the eye" warning is not the first warning that the Holy Spirit gave in the dream. Indeed, it took me a while to realize that it is in fact the third warning during the final moments of the Rapture itself.

Knowing that the Rapture itself, or rather the ascension itself, is going to take just 100 to 150 milliseconds, the first and second warnings became clear to me. So what are they? The first is this:

The Lord will give us a presentiment that the Rapture is imminent. The first warning on the day of the Rapture itself is a feeling that it is going to happen. However, the spiritual heads-up, the nod from God the Spirit, will only come if you are in a relationship with Christ. Only.

Remember what I wrote about the vision? "As I spoke to my father, I had this strong feeling that the Rapture was about to happen, that I was about to be taken." Now, this presentiment of the Rapture could only have come from the Holy Spirit.

He is the Spirit of Christ, He is today my First and Greatest Love, my closest friend, my guide, my teacher, my counselor, my interpreter, my reminder, my organizer, my healing, my liberation, my source of spiritual and emotional health, my warning sign, my power in Jesus Christ.

He is everything for my Lord God is my shepherd and I shall not want, providing me daily with what I need, He carries my daily burdens and supports me throughout the day, accompanying me wherever I go as I talk to others. It is to whom I speak to first and last every day, my good morning, my good night, my source of prayer and who talks through me to others. I digress but you get the point.

So, let's go back to the last point, the Spirit of God, had given me the presentiment, or rather a heads-up through my spirit that the Rapture was about to happen. We need to understand that the first warning is not the bright lights but a very concrete feeling that the Rapture is about to happen. In other words, the Holy Spirit warns us first to get ready because the Rapture is coming.

Obviously, this is very important. You would imagine that everyone would want a heads-up ahead of the biggest moment in his or her life, right? As I had previously mentioned, did the Lord not warn Noah decades before the flood itself or Lot the night before He destroyed Sodom and Gomorrah?

Noah and Lot lived in a righteous relationship with our Lord God. They walked with the Lord. They received heads-ups too! We are also called to walk with the Lord and live in a relationship with Him. I will reiterate this, those who are truly in Christ, who have a living relationship with our living and risen God in the sky, will know beforehand that the Rapture will happen just moments before it happens. Relationship matters, however, how long do we have between receiving the presentiment of the imminent Rapture before the actual event itself?

This is a great question. Here is another question that we could just as easily ask, how long do we have to alert our closest loved ones before the Rapture comes? What I can say is that we will at least have enough time to call a relative like I did in my vision. Yes, I called my father to ask him to confess his sins.

Remember I couldn't hear the conversation, I didn't hear what he had to say to me but it is clear to me that he responded one way or the other as I watched the amber and bright whitish yellow lights outside on the whitish wall with no windows.

This conversation also helped me to understand the timing better. How? Well, it takes at least 33 to 40 seconds to dial someone on a smartphone and connect (this includes reaching out to the phone by the side). On top of this, I also had time to ask my father to confess his sins – I have no idea whether we were already talking at that point, there is that, and whether I said, "hey dad, how are you?" But given that I already had a presentiment of the Rapture, I would not have wasted time with chit chat and would have gone straight to the point (I write this in the past knowing that this will happen in the future, just bear with me as I work through this).

You see, it takes little to realize that my father and I would have already had time to have discussed the Rapture years before it happens.

So, let's do some back-of-the-envelope calculations here. We are talking of at least 20 seconds that we can be sure of – this includes the moment of asking my father twice to confess his sins to Jesus (taking approximately 6 seconds), listening to his reply (at least 10 seconds) while watching the lights outside, then feeling the disappointment I did in the vision and afterward saying, "it is now, it is now" (3 seconds).

At this point, everything moves a lot faster with the Fire of God descending (1 second or so) and am taken up (100-150 milliseconds according to the time marker left by Paul in 1 Corinthians 15). When we include the time it takes to dial someone and that person pick up, we can add at least another 33 to 40 seconds.

Consequently, we are talking about a minimum of 53 seconds between the presentiment of the Rapture, picking up a phone, calling someone and then the Fire of God coming down and taking everybody up. This is not much time for anybody.

When you consider that the timing above is based on ideal conditions, we may have approximately a minute or more before the end. Either way, we have to be quick on our toes, confess our sins, forgive whoever there is to forgive and see if there are others who will need some form of support at this moment too.

Indeed, it is important to remember that when this moment comes, we confess our sins, and say something fast and simple such as "Jesus, forgive me of the sins I remember and do not remember, and those I do not know." And if there is someone to forgive still, then this would absolutely be the time to say: "Lord I also forgive such and such person for what he/she or they did to me." That is it. No one goes up if he or she has not forgiven others for the hurt they have caused and it is also key we confess our sins one last time – just to make sure!

Ultimately, it is critically important that we all have a habit of confessing our sins daily and renewing our faith in Christ. This is a key part of being in a relationship with Christ. This makes it easier and faster the next time when we must confess our sins.

When we do this every morning, we need only think on the sins of the past day.

But what about the rest of the family or very close friends at that last moment? I believe that by the time of the Rapture, family, friends as well as brothers and sisters in Christ will all be in organized messaging groups with some kind of alert mechanism in place – like a final message and how to confess sins quickly. I am not kidding.

This is a big deal, because the Rapture is going to happen. Does not the Bible say be prepared before the end? Has this message not been given time and time again in church? It is time for all of us to take this issue very seriously. After all, how do you prepare for travel? Do you not tell colleagues at work and ensure workflows continue while you are out? And what about family? Do you not let them know that you are heading to Greece or Mexico? And if they are going with you, do you not pack ahead of time and get ready?

Well, the journey of the Rapture is far more special. The wonderful thing is that you get to take nothing – so no worries there, however, you only go if you are in a relationship with the Lord. And if that is not an issue because you are in one, what about the others in your life at work or at home that are not in a relationship with Christ?

How you position others about Christ is a personal choice, but all Christians are under the command to tell others about Jesus. And if you already know that you are going to be raptured because you are in a relationship with the Lord (you pray and read the Bible daily, and go to church weekly), but there are those around you who are not – think on that, think of the consequences for those people around you.

Imagine, if there are people in your midst – colleagues that you have worked with for years and years, and you never told them once about Christ and they all end up in an eternal fiery hell. The Lord will call you out on this on Judgement Day. It is important to reach out to others. We have a number of years just yet but planning for that last day is a big deal and should not be taken lightly.

So, the key message here and by far the most important one that I can impart in this whole book is that you need to be in a relationship with Christ not only to be saved but to also know that the Rapture itself is going to happen before it takes place. It is critically important for so many reasons that we all receive the Holy Spirit's heads-up that the Rapture is imminent.

However, and this is a hypothetical example but a very possible situation, if for some reason in the future it is the day of the Rapture and you will have read this book but you did not receive a presentiment of the coming Rapture from the Holy Spirit, and someone tells you that the Rapture is coming, then you need to get on your knees there and then, and start asking for forgiveness for your sins because you do not want to be left behind.

You do not want to have to deal with the ensuing tribulation. You will not be able to handle it. The Rapture will be devastating. Christ revealed as much at the end of this book!

Now, let's look at this Rapture warning in more depth - if you are reading this, and are not yet in Christ, or you are baptized but not in a relationship with Christ, I can tell you that the chances are that you will not receive the spiritual pre-warning or presentiment about the imminent Rapture from the Holy Spirit unless you are in a relationship with Christ.

This is the most important message or rather warning about the Rapture to unbelievers and the unchurched, who are made up of baptized Christians who no longer go to church. We must be in a relationship with Christ because then you will know that the Rapture is coming, and if you know the Rapture is coming you can warn others and be used by the Lord in the last moments to try to save others because if you are not in a relationship, you will not receive the pre-warning from the Holy Spirit, you will not know to look out of the window for a sign and you will certainly not be prepared for that last moment of your life as you know it on earth.

The Rapture will happen before your eyes and you will be left behind. It may feel that I am going in circles on this point. I only do so because there is nothing more important than salvation.

If people's spiritual eyes were opened and they could see the demons in supermarkets, street corners, public transport, schools and in their own homes camped in the living rooms or bedrooms, they would jump off of their sofas and run to their nearest church, asking for forgiveness along the way!

Just today alone, approximately 150,000 people have died worldwide, or more than 26 million deaths so far in the first six months of 2024 (January 1 to June 7).

How many of those went to hell and how many to heaven? Far more are going down than up. This is why there is no such thing as the gospel of the tomorrow in the Bible – anywhere – the time to get into a relationship with Christ is today, not tomorrow. Procrastination or wicked stubbornness, self-righteousness or an undying love for sin have all been the undoing of so many.

Let me explain this more clearly. If a Christian is unchurched or has stopped frequenting a church but is a believer who prays now and again to the Lord, and perhaps goes to church once a year, and thinks that he or she is going to be saved on the day of the Rapture, then I can tell you that that person is not in a relationship with Christ.

Here is the problem, and most people do not realize this, but the day a Christian stops going to church, he or she has just lost a spiritual battle that that person did not even realize he or she was in. The Holy Spirit has shown me the Lord inviting His people back to church time and time again – but most recently, I saw the Lord with His arm thrust forward and His hand open, calling a believer to return to church just eight days after he had been to his last Sunday service. Eight days only!

The Lord wants us all to pick up our crosses and commit – this includes going to church every week because He made a heck of a statement on the Cross and went all out for all of us. He paid a bill that we cannot. That person may certainly not feel that he or she is out of relationship with Christ after eight days, may not even agree with such a statement, but this is what the Holy Spirit showed me during prayer, surprising me in the process as the Holy Spirit also shows Jesus making the same gesture of outstretched arm and open hand, inviting folk who have stopped going to church for years.

What I do know is that the Lord sets the bar high, He knows our future, is more than aware of the spiritual risks that we typically cannot see and expects us to go to church weekly because this is after all the least that we can do.

You see, when a person is unchurched, he or she is spiritually out of position, and that is dangerous because that soul is spiritually vulnerable if not rapidly being spiritually compromised. Only a fellow brother or sister in Christ with discernment of spirits and spiritual authority will know how to best deal with such a situation and pray for a lost unchurched soul so that the Holy Spirit comes and quickens him or her (brings the Christian back to spiritual life).

Now, here is another layer of complexity. The Lord will keep sending His servants to bring such unchurched folk back to church. However, if such a person does not return and ignores the Lord's invites, sometimes Christ will simply remove His support from that soul and either he or she will find himself or herself in stormy waters, or worse yet receive a scare so great that the unchurched Christian runs back to church.

However, if the situation is hopeless, that person could lose his or her life because the Lord knows that he or she will never come back to Him and that He has been completely rejected. It is a morbid view but does it not say:

"In due time their foot will slip (Deuteronomy 32:35 NIV)?"

I am not judging others here, the point is to warn others because the Lord has shown me again and again that Jesus is calling His people back to Him before it is too late, and I know that He will use his servants to keep telling others to come back to Christ right up to the very end, indeed, right up to the last minute before the Rapture itself.

For me, it is hard to understand why people would not want to invest in their eternity. Folk get so worked up about putting money into pensions, equities and bonds, so why would you not want to invest in eternity – really, why would someone not be bothered about living in a hell hole with Satan or worse yet in a lake of sulfur and fire with other tormented souls and demons for all time?

Seriously, that is not fun, that is eternal punishment and there is no way out of there, no way back. Have you made a decision between feeling the Lord's fury for all eternity or knowing His peace, joy and righteousness in His Kingdom of God?

Now, let's return to the vision and the timing of the Rapture and the last minute of our genuinely Christian lives on earth! When the first shimmering amber-yellow-white lights shine outside, everyone has less than 10 seconds to react. What will you do? Will you say, "Jesus forgive me for my sins, while I forgive others and turn over all grudges to you Lord?" Or will you be busy alerting others around you and say, "the Rapture is now, it is now, get ready!" Either way, you just do not have much time.

So, the second warning is that there will be bright amber-yellow-white lights shimmering on the walls, streets, hills around the world. The Fire of God will fall on earth, and we have just 10 seconds left before departure (or not).

It seems such little time at this point, just 10 odd seconds to go before the big moment. As I write this, the Holy Spirit told me why we have so little time in terms of heads-up and that is because the Rapture itself is so fast.

Remember, Sodom & Gomorrah was destroyed over the course of a day – how many hours, we cannot know but the warning to Lot and his family came the night before. Noah had more than a century of a heads-up.

Why? He needed time to build the vessel, true, but he also spent more than a year in the ark before a dove returned with an olive leaf. The Rapture itself happens in the blink of an eye, so it seems reasonable, if we apply respectively Lot's and Noah's examples of a day and a year, to expect that there is a minute or so of a warning from the Lord before the big event takes place within the blink of an eye.

There is, if you will, a form of divine symmetry behind this all. So, what we can know from the vison and the basic calculations done earlier in the chapter, is that we have some 53 seconds to a minute or so of warning before the Rapture.

This is little time to be prepared, little time to confess our sins and forgive, little time to warn others, little time to say those final farewells, little time to look each other in the eye and say "I love you," before waiting for the lights and then saying "for your glory Lord" as the bright amber Fire of God descends and takes us up.

So, when church leaders around the world say "be ready for the Rapture," or be "ready for when the Lord Jesus comes back," or be "ready for the end," they are not kidding. The two separate moments of the Rapture and the arrival of Jesus' second "coming with the clouds (Revelation 1:7)" will come upon the world fast and those of the world will not know what hit them until it is too late. The Rapture will catch out so many baptized out of relationship Christians! Will it be tens of millions that will be left behind? Hundreds of millions?

We can never know. Indeed, during prayer in the Spirit, I asked the Lord just how many would be impacted by the Rapture, and His response was this: *"What matters is that people take heed, change their lives, for time is running out."* So, take heed!

We must be prepared and help others to be prepared too for the Rapture will come first and then Christ will come with the clouds: "*For you don't know what day your Lord is coming. [43] Understand this: If a homeowner knew exactly when a burglar was coming, he would keep watch and not permit his house to be broken into. [44] You also must be ready all the time, for the Son of Man will come when least expected (Matthew 42b-44 NLT).*"

The Rapture will be a day of celebration for God's people in the sky but it will also be a day of great sadness. I am sure those who go up will reflect solemnly on the loved ones who were not raptured. I know that on this day the Holy Spirit will be joyous but knowing Him as I have come to know Him in Spirit during prayer, He will also be deeply aggrieved – for He often shows me His great sadness when I meet those unchurched souls who have stopped going to church and yet think they are okay because they pray once or twice a week.

The Holy Spirit fills me with the same sadness and tears, stirring in me the compassion that He doubtless feels for all of the Lord's people who are lost. As an evangelist, this moves me and motivates me deeply to pray more, fast more and talk more about the Lord to others.

For Jesus never said to God the Father, "Well Father, I am going to the Cross, to suffer the most horrible of deaths, so people can ignore me." No, instead, Jesus agreed to go to the Cross because God the Father made a promise to God the Son,

'[27] My sheep listen to my voice; I know them, and they follow me. [28] I give them eternal life, and they shall never perish; no one will snatch them out of my

hand. [29] *My Father, who has given them to me, is greater than all; no one can snatch them out of my Father's hand.* [30] *I and the Father are one (John 10:27-30 NIV)."*

No one can snatch the Lord's people out of the Heavenly Father's hand. However, our Lord God has also given us free will. He respects this greatly and He will not interfere with someone's will – for the Lord too wants to be loved freely and not because we feel coerced into loving Him. Coercion, emotional blackmail, or anything that is in any way forceful, is not the way of the Lord.

What I do know is that the Holy Spirit has told me that I will speak to many but not all will come, and that I should be prepared for much disappointment. He wasn't kidding! It is little wonder that we are called sheep, for the moment, we pull an unchurched sheep out of a ditch, more often than not, that same sheep still finds his or her way back into another ditch, and yet again becomes stuck! The price of free will is great and only in the next life will we understand the full extent of its cost.

So let's recap, the Rapture is going to be fast, we will have 53 seconds or possibly more to act (Holy Spirit warning I), we will see amber-yellowish shimmering lights outside (warning II), then they will disappear and we will have just seconds before we are enveloped in His glorious Fire of God and taken up within 100-150 milliseconds (warning III because we will not have time to react, for at that moment, it is done).

We need to be ready, we need to be in a relationship with Jesus Christ. There are no loopholes. And there is no point in trying to deceive ourselves or others about our own relationship with Christ – the Lord knows and judges our hearts.

∂If you dear reader have not yet made a decision about Christ, then reach out today, and ask the Lord to come into your heart and show you! For there is no gospel of tomorrow in the Bible. It is important to act today. And if you are already baptized but are in a struggling relationship, struggling is okay because it is still a relationship!

However, if you are spiritually dead, then the advice is the same to the person who is struggling and that is reach out to Christ and get closer to the Lord for He will get closer to you (James 4:8). This supernatural law never fails! Make the effort, seek the Lord and keep seeking, keep praying and keep pushing because if you are not feeling Christ in your life, it is because you are not making the necessary effort to be close enough to Him.

The closer a person gets, the more incredible the relationship is! Seconds of prayer do not count. That said, praying a few minutes in the morning, reading a few verses of the Bible, and finishing the day in prayer – as well as attending church weekly, is one way to getting started and developing new and deeper spiritual habits with time.

So, is that it, just three warnings? No, there is still the antichrist to address but more importantly, how can we really be sure that this is going to happen in the coming years? What did the vision reveal about this and how does Matthew 24 help?

Chapter 6
Noah and my father

[36] "But about that day or hour no one knows, not even the angels in heaven, nor the Son, but only the Father. [37] As it was in the days of Noah, so it will be at the coming of the Son of Man (Matthew 24:36-37 NIV)."

The initial idea of this chapter was to tell it through the eyes of Matthew and Peter following Jesus' discourse on the Mount of Olives and how that connects us directly to the Rapture, the return of our Lord and the end of all things. Exciting, no? Instead, it is important to invert this chapter so that you dear reader can understand why Jesus' Olivet Discourse really matters to all of us and helps us understand the timing of the Rapture thanks to an important detail that was also revealed in the June 12 vision.

What could that be? Well, firstly, we need to understand the nature of a Holy Spirit dream or vision. You see, if you ask any servant of the Lord or any theologian, they will tell you that every vision received from the Holy Spirit is personal in nature. And the vision that the Holy Spirit gave me was no exception to that rule.

The key personal elements include my presence in the vision, my father on the phone, the family that I could not see in my future study, the fact that I will be in an English church building on the last day and not at home (wherever that will be because I currently live in Brazil and not England), the absence of my wife and children (something that I have not yet figured out though my wife is always busy and my children will almost all if not all will be adults by the end)!

However, the key factor in all of these personal details is my father. Dad is ironically the key to the timing of the Rapture in more ways than one. Really. For the Lord did not put before me a calendar or a ticking clock to tell me when the end will come. No, that would not have been Biblical.

I would have discarded the dream and would never have written this book. For we are not supposed to know when the Rapture will happen or when Christ is coming back.

So many theologians have dedicated years trying to answer the question of when, and I trust that they were fruitful, however, the Holy Father has never wanted us to know the timing of the ending and that has not changed.

That said, the Holy Spirit provided me with a vital clue in the dream and that is my father. Dad turns 78 years old in 2024. Why does this matter? The vision shows that my dad is still alive when the Rapture happens.

He has amazing health, seen many battles as a war correspondent and led an incredible life. Consequently, we can safely assume that the Rapture will happen at some point within the next 20-odd years. Can we pinpoint the timing further? I can but that is deeply private.

However, there is more. Something very important is going to happen in the next decade and that is the 2,000th anniversary of the crucifixion, resurrection and ascension of our Lord Jesus Christ.

This time will also mark the 2,000th anniversary of the year that the Holy Spirit inaugurated the church at Pentecost. Why does that matter? To some folk this question is offensive because it is obvious as to why it matters, however, it is not that apparent to everybody. So, let's go deeper into this issue.

Anyone who knows the Lord knows that Adonai Elohim loves symmetry. If you take the Bible, you have Creation at the start and you have New Creation at the end and the tree of life is both in the garden of Eden (Genesis 2) and in the Kingdom of God (Revelation 22)! And what is in between Creation and New Creation? Jesus. Symmetry. This is basic theology.

Another example is the gap between Genesis and Exodus, and Malachi (the last prophet in the Old Testament) and the gospel of Matthew, which starts the New Testament.

Both gaps are marked by a period of approximately 400 years. During this time between Genesis and Exodus (birth of Moses) and Malachi and Matthew (birth of Jesus), there were no miracles, no prophets, in short, nothing of note was recorded, and then, there was an explosion of activity from the Lord – the 10 plagues over Egypt and the parting of the Red Sea in Exodus, and in Matthew, miracle after miracle from the Lord Jesus Christ.

The two periods are the most intense in terms of activity from the Lord. Again, symmetry. On top of this, Jesus relived key moments of Exodus during His 3.5-year ministry. How so? N.T. Wright in his work Simply Jesus makes this point best, noting how there are seven core elements that mark the ministry of Christ and the Exodus from Egypt.

They are a wicked tyrant (Pharoah in Exodus versus Caesar in the four gospels), a chosen leader (Moses and Jesus), a rescue by sacrifice (the blood of the lamb versus the perfect sacrificial Lamb), a new vocation and way of life (Mosaic Law versus a new covenant in Christ's blood Luke 22:19-20), the presence of God (the mounts, cloud and pillar of fire versus the transfiguration of Jesus, His baptism, and walking on water) and lastly the promised and inherited land.

Moses led the Israelites to the promised land (though he was under the commands of Jesus), and it is Jesus who is the Exodus of salvation for all who come to Him.

Wright states: "*Since Jesus himself seems to have deliberately chosen the Exodus story, the Passover story as the setting for the carefully stated climax to his own public career, it's important that we think for a moment about the seven great features of this story, which all first-century Jews would have known in their bones. All this – we are still learning to take off our modern Western spectacles and put on first-century Jewish ones! – is essential if we are to understand what Jesus thought he was doing. If we don't get this straight, we shall simply squash Jesus into the little boxes of our own imaginations rather than seeing him as he was (N.T. Wright, Simply Jesus p.63-64).*"

And the similarities do not stop there. Remembering that Moses appeared with Elijah at the Transfiguration of Jesus (Matthew 17:1-8), Jesus spent 40 days in the desert fasting while the Israelites wandered the wilderness for 40 years, and then came that day when the Israelites' crossed the Jordan river into the promised land (Joshua 3:1). Jesus's ministry began when he was baptized in the Jordan (Matthew 3:13), for He is the promised land and inheritance!

Ultimately, there are many more examples and this all proves that the Lord loves symmetry! It would not be that much of a leap to think that Jesus is coming back 2,000 years after his resurrection! This is the hope among so many of the Lord's servants.

However, there is a detail here, in fact there are some loose ends that have many of us stumped for it would be really easy for us to say that Jesus is coming back in 2033 but wait, was it in AD33 or AD30 that Jesus was crucified and resurrected? And if we do not know if it was one year or the other, who is to say that it was not AD31, AD32, or AD34?

Most, like Life Application Study Bible NLT and the Holman Illustrated Bible Dictionary, put the resurrection at AD30, whereas theologians argue it could just as easily be AD33 or at the very latest AD34.

Whatever the year is, we have little time left to evangelize the unbelievers and re-evangelize the unchurched, but could it all be so soon? And what more evidence can we really gather to confirm that we are at the end?

Cue dad again! He is 77, almost 78 at this point in 2024, and thank the Maker that my father has never had any serious health issues during his life and is still with us. If anything, I have seen the Lord's hand in protecting my father again and again throughout the decades as a war correspondent from the Northern Ireland Troubles in 1970, to reporting behind enemy lines from Buenos Aires during the Falklands conflict in 1982, and when he twice went into Iraq in 1990 and 2003 with British troops. And what about the time he disappeared for three days in Mostar during the Yugoslav conflict? This is an excerpt in my father's words about what happened in 1993:

"The "kidnap" incident was less dramatic than it might sound. During the Yugoslav conflict the Bosnian city of Mostar was under siege for most of 1992 to 1994. In the latter stages Bosnian Croats, former allies of the Bosniaks, waged a cruel campaign with artillery and sniper fire. More than 2,000 mostly civilians died. In the high summer of 1993 (I think that was the year) the UN reached an agreement to send in a desperately needed aid convoy. I went in on the back of a lorry and after some delays managed to file a story about the truly horrific situation - no food, medicine or power. Water came from the river which was watched by snipers. The next day the military commander (not really a warlord) announced that the convoy would not be allowed to leave.

The idea was that while the UN aid workers were there the Croats would not keep shooting. That proved to be an unreal hope. We were effectively hostages. Eventually after three days a woman called Sally Becker told me she knew a route out of the city and was going to guide an American film crew. There was room in the vehicle for me. Sally is a remarkable person. Her humanitarian work during that conflict earned her many honors including a Nobel Prize nomination. She was dubbed the Angel of Mostar for her efforts to helping people there. We crammed into the vehicle and following Sally's instructions got out without being shot at. It allowed me to file a front-page piece for the London Evening Standard. I cannot read about the horrors of Gaza without thinking of what I witnessed in Sarajevo and Mostar. God help those people. With love, as always – dad."

I am sure the Lord has dispatched quite a few angels to my father's rescue without him ever knowing so! For this is how the Lord works – nothing is ever a coincidence or good fortune or just plain luck. Have you ever given thanks to the Lord for the number of times He has rescued you from a tricky situation, financial suicide, a vice, depression or even death itself? Did He ever bring you back from the brink of suicide?

The Lord has many a time come to my rescue from appendicitis as a boy, pancreatitis as an adult, or that COVID-19 jab that left my heart racing and my head nearly ready to explode two days after I had blacked out.

Jesus also "fixed" my mother's health last year and said He saved one of my daughters when she was in the womb. This is what He said about my daughter: *"She was going to die but She is mine, no one takes from Me what is Mine, for I have plans for her and I saved her."* My daughter was born with one kidney. We can never know the million and one things that the Lord does, or will do, or why He does them when He does them and for what purpose. He is awesome. We can just be grateful that we are still here and have purpose!

Now, going back to the vision and my father. Why is he so important? Here is the thing, my father is currently 77. That means he was born in 1946. It is important to remember this year because we are going to go into the Bible and examine further the so-called Noah generation and its connection to dad. But what is this Noah generation? Are we talking about the Noah generation that died in the flood? Yes and no.

It is important to know that the Noah generation is in fact the name that Jesus gave to the last generation of humanity on earth. It is a generation that happens twice in the history of humanity, a generation that is marked by two planetary-wide calamities – the first time, there was a flood and the second, a fiery finish for all on the Day of the Lord when the elements will melt!

Interestingly, a key characteristic of this Noah generation is that the people were oblivious to what was happening around them just before the flood. They were also violent and unrepentant. The next Noah generation is expected to be the same. Here is a question, are we not seeing this all over again in 2024?

Allow me to make this bold statement and cut straight to the chase. We are part of the Noah generation, which most likely started in the 1940s or the 1930s, and on top of that, time is running out. I may seem to be out on a limb at this point but am I?

Really? To reach the same conclusion as me (that we are indeed of this final Noah generation), it is important to understand it better and ask ourselves what the 1940s have anything to do with Matthew 24, otherwise known as the Olivet Discourse, and 2 Peter 2 and 3. Indeed, how can we be sure?

Matthew 24 is arguably one of the most important texts to be written on the last days in the Bible. In summary, Jesus says in Matthew 24 that all of the end times prophecies will happen within the same period of one generation – a generation that He calls the Noah generation. Jesus lists the prophecies and describes the Noah generation so that we can identify it. However, our Lord denies us critical information as to when the end itself will come. He does not provide a date. No one knows when Jesus will come back, for example.

When the disciples asked the Lord about the day when He will return, Jesus replied that about *"that day or hour no one knows, not even the angels in heaven, nor the Son, but only the Father (Matthew 24:36 NIV)."* We should not be dismayed with this response. Christ in His infinite wisdom clearly did not give us a date for His return, He was not explicit about the timing around the Rapture either and He did not provide us a date as to when planet earth will meet its cataclysmic demise ahead of New Creation!

Can you imagine how society would have restructured itself if Jesus had provided such dates? How the world would be different, just picture the panic, depression, media or films around such events? Better not to know, better to keep us on our feet, better for us to live this day now to the fullest, better to fix our eyes on Jesus and know that we must keep asking, keep seeking and keep knocking so that we grow, grow, grow in Christ!

Thankfully we are spared the dates but we must still keep our eyes peeled for the signs that indicate whether we are part of the Noah generation or not.

This is why the Olivet Discourse in Matthew 24 is so important as it highlights persecution, the second coming of Christ and the Rapture. We see similar texts in Mark 13, Luke 21 with smatterings between Luke 12-20. Peter also refers to the Olivet Discourse indirectly and provides some pointers about the Rapture in 2 Peter 2, which we will come to after dissecting Matthew 24. Luke and Mark, however, make no reference to Noah but state that all of the last days signs will happen during the course of one generation, which according to the Bible lasts up to 100 years (Genesis 15:13-16).

So how can we identify this so-called Noah generation and know we are a part of it for sure? To do this we need to understand the signs prophesied by Christ in Matthew 24.

Jesus had left the temple when the disciples came up to him to "call his attention to its buildings (verse 1)." This prompts Jesus to respond that "not one stone here will be left on another (verse 2)." Later, the disciples come up to Jesus on the Mount of Olives to ask Him "when will this happen, and what will be the sign of your coming and of the end of the age (verse 3)?" The disciples - including Matthew and Peter - want to know more about the destruction of the second Temple.

Christ kicks off the Olivet discourse and lists the prophecies, stating there will be wars and rumors of wars (verse 6); nations rise against nations, famines and earthquakes (verse 7); persecution and hatred of Christians by all nations (verse 9); apostasy with many giving up on Christianity amid betrayal and hatred toward each other (verse 10); many false prophets will appear and deceive many people (verse 11); an increase in wickedness while the love of most will grow cold (verse 12); and that lastly, the Gospel of the Kingdom will be preached worldwide to all nations (verse 14) before the end comes.

Of this list, most people will be quick to say that wars, famines and earthquakes have been around since Jesus, so what? Persecution has also been around since the beginning – Jesus went to the Cross for starters, Stephen was stoned to death (Acts 7:54-60), James, whose brother John was exiled to the island of Patmos, was beheaded (Acts 12:2) while Peter was arrested shortly afterward and was set for trial but was freed by an angel.

Saul of Tarsus persecuted the Church at the start, he "*was uttering threats with every breath and was eager to kill the Lord's followers (Acts 9:10 NIV),*" before he himself was converted and was renamed Paul, who in turn suffered all types of attacks, from physical to verbal as well as imprisonment before being executed.

All disciples came to an untimely demise after heading abroad to different parts of the earth. The Bible does not record each of their deaths but other documents state that they all met gruesome deaths from beheadings to crucifixion and boiling oil.

For sure all of the disciples ended up drinking from the cup of the Lord (Matthew 20:22-23) as Jesus had predicted. Simply put, persecution has dogged the church since Jesus went to the cross and it has not stopped since but Matthew 24:9 verse states that there will be hatred and persecution of Christians *"by all nations"* at the end. Are we there yet?

In 2021, 360 million Christians were persecuted worldwide with Afghanistan leading the list of offending countries in terms of violence, attacks and hate crimes, according to Strasbourg-based association Portes Ouvertes, wrote French publication Ouest-France in January 2022.

In that same article, the daily reported that the number of Christians who were killed for their faith jumped 24% to 5,898 deaths in 2021 across 76 countries, according to French group Fédération Protestante de France. More than 80% of these deaths were across Africa.

Moreover, more than 15% of the world's 2.36 billion Christians worldwide face persecution. It is hard to imagine 360 million people facing persecution and I would imagine that the numbers are far worse. So, are we seeing today what Jesus prophesied in Matthew 24:9 - hatred and persecution of Christians *"by all nations"*? Whatever answer I give would be subjective.

There is no statistic that can prove this either, however, you need only look at the state of the world today. Anti-Christianism is widespread across developed and developing nations. The US and Brazil have more Christians than any other nation in the world, and yet believers and pastors in both countries are increasingly under attack from government authorities. So, if the prophetic sign spelled out by Jesus in Matthew 24 is not already here, then we can be certain that we are very close to such a reality.

So, what about apostasy, which involves Christians rejecting their faith in Christ? This has been an issue since the very start of Christianity (John 6:66 and 2 Timothy 4:9-10).

However, who could possibly know how many hundreds of millions of Christians have given up their rights to eternal life in Christ in the 21st century? It is hard to know just how grave this situation is worldwide.

In a 2020 Gallup poll, the number of US adults that belonged to a church was below 50% for the first in eight decades of research, totaling just 47%. Gallup noted that US church membership was at 73% in 1937 and remained at nearly 70% for the next six decades before starting to decline steadily from 2008 onwards.

The Gallup poll shows a significant decline in the number of Christians among millennials (36%) versus generation X (50%) and baby boomers (58%). So, this poll shows that apostasy is rising, however, what is driving this problem?

Is this because Christians are giving up because they do not see the Lord's fire in the church that they frequent?

Obviously, this is not what the Lord God wants for any of us because the mission is His and no one else's, and many must be saved!

What is clear is that we need to move toward a show and tell Gospel format of the church. The kind where people can know that Christ is very much in their lives, and that their church is brimming with the presence of the Lord. Indeed, we need more churches confirmed by signs and wonders – miracles of all kinds from healings to prophecy and deliverance from demonic oppression.

Churches where the Kingdom of God comes down to the congregation and hearts are healed, lives are restored, forgiveness supplants bitterness, and people know who Jesus really is! In short, churches where the Kingdom of God is not only preached but practiced! After all, are we not called to imitate Christ (Ephesians 5:1)? This includes imitating His ministry too! For the Kingdom of God is why Jesus Christ came.

It is what He preached and what He practiced. Indeed, He inaugurated the Kingdom of God on the Cross. Christ is the embodiment of the attributes that the Kingdom of God has to offer – peace, joy and righteousness. This generation needs to hear the Good News and see it confirmed with signs and wonders! We must all pray for this and for each church to be filled with the presence of the Lord.

However, what do we see every week? Churches attacking other churches. There is church in-fighting within the same denomination as well as mudslinging between churches of different denominations!

We can see pastors openly attacking others on YouTube and other social media channels as well as on the news. This is in part what Matthew meant when he wrote the word *"betray"* in 24:10 NIV: *"At that time many will turn away from the faith and will betray and hate each other."*

And this is everything Paul warned against (2 Corinthians 10:10-13) and everything that the devil loves to see happen. Why? Whoever criticizes a church pastor is attacking the delegated authority that the Lord vested in that person and is consequently attacking God Himself.

There are countless examples in the Bible about why this should not happen – just check out Numbers 12, 14, 16 as well as Romans 13:1-5 and Romans 14:4. What are the sheep to think? The criticisms and in-fighting need to stop for the Lord needs an army of servants to seek His presence above all, to minister to Him first, to praise and worship Him, to hunger and thirst for Him, to pray at all times in the Spirit, and to be guided by the Holy Spirit under His divine authority.

Such servants must also preach the Good News and the promises of the Kingdom of God before a repentant congregation that also yearns for His presence but fears the Lord! Until that happens, pastors will just give up and quit and thousands of churches will close every year.

Sadly, this has never been so prevalent as in the 2020s, for even lawlessness has overrun the church. Just google the words "pastor arrested" and you will see news about such situations occurring at a different church every couple of days in the US alone. It is far from encouraging and the allegations are diverse from child molestation to rape, drugs and prostitution rings. However, these events are all a sign of the end times.

"Now we beseech you, brethren, by the coming of our Lord Jesus Christ, and by our gathering together unto him, [2] That ye be not soon shaken in mind, or be troubled, neither by spirit, nor by word, nor by letter as from us, as that the day of Christ is at hand. [3] Let no man deceive you by any means: for that day shall not come, except there come a falling away first, and that man of sin be revealed, the son of perdition (2 Thessalonians 2:1-4 KJV)."

Notice the use of the words *"falling away first."* In other versions, this apostasy or great falling away is described as a "*great rebellion against God* (NLT)," or as The Message version of the Bible writes: "*Before that day* (of Christ) *comes, a couple of things have to happen. First, the Apostasy. Second, the debt of the Anarchist, a partner in crime with Satan.*" Note, how apostasy has become Apostasy. So, all of this has to happen! More and more churches will abandon the Lord's values or just give up and throw in the towel because it is prophesied! But what other factors are at play?

Let's continue with Matthew, who wrote in verse 24:11, "[11] *and many false prophets will appear and deceive many people.*" So, the great apostasy can only really happen if there are false prophets.

Typically, a false prophet is interested in self-promotion and financial gain. We see this often when such folk offer prosperity or healing to Christians if donations are made to their cause, for example. Simon the Sorcerer in Acts 8:9-25 is an example of a type of false prophet, who offered Peter and John money to receive the Spirit so that he could benefit afterward.

'20 Peter answered: "May your money perish with you, because you thought you could buy the gift of God with money! 21 You have no part or share in this ministry, because your heart is not right before God. 22 Repent of this wickedness and pray to the Lord in the hope that he may forgive you for having such a thought in your heart. 23 For I see that you are full of bitterness and captive to sin (Acts 8:20-23 NIV)."

Simon's plans were nipped in the bud. However, false prophets continue to this day and they are more prevalent than ever before. For me, the worst kind of false prophet is the one who denies Christ's divinity. Have you ever had a discussion with someone who firmly believes that Christ is not the Lord but almost believes in everything else that a Christian does?

Such a person will be quick to take you to Hebrews 1:6 to say that Jesus is the creation of our Heavenly Father because "*God brings his firstborn into the world.*"

Could Jesus really be part of God's creation and not the risen and living God sitting at the righthand side of the Heavenly Father? Is Christ created as opposed to Creator?

Colossians 1:18 NIV, however, clearly states that Jesus is the *"head of the body, the church, he is the beginning and the firstborn from among the dead, so that in all things He might have the preeminence."* The emphasis here is that Christ is the *"beginning,"* the first, the firstborn and preeminent, or as the NLT (New Living Translation) version of the Bible states, Jesus is the "*first in everything.*"

Christ is not created, He is the "*beginning,*" and where do we first see the word "*beginning*" in the Bible? That answer is Genesis 1:1, where we learn that *"In the beginning, God created the heavens and the earth."*

It is very interesting to note that God is Elohim in the Hebrew and original version of Genesis 1:1. Elohim means God in the masculine plural. You see, Jesus was there in the beginning, creating and not being created, for the Father, the Holy Spirit and the Son are all present in the first three verses of Genesis 1:1-3!

Paul the Apostle, who wrote Colossians and most likely wrote the book of Hebrews, is making a clear reference between Jesus and God by stating that Christ is the beginning, for He is the risen Lord! So why does this all matter? Paul is making it clear that Jesus is the beginning (of creation) and that He is the firstborn among the dead. He is not created but is the Creator.

But wait a minute, Hebrews 1:6 states that God brought Christ back to life. If Christ were truly divine, He would have brought Himself back to life, no? In fact, it was not only the Heavenly Father, who brought Christ back to life (Acts 2:24), but also the Holy Spirit (1 Peter 3:18) and Christ too (John 2:19, 10:18).

The Father, the Spirit and Christ all resurrected Christ. How come? Remember Elohim? Our Lord is the triune God of the universe, He is three persons in one – inseparable and in perfect unity. Our triune God moves as One. Remember Isaiah 58:14 NLT where it states, *"I, the Lord, have spoken!"* We also see this in Genesis 18, when *"The Lord appeared to Abraham (v1)... Abraham looked up and saw three men standing nearby (v2)... "very well," they answered, "do as you say (v5).""*

In other words, God appeared as three men to Abraham and spoke in unison – for the Lord moves as One in perfect Trinity unity. On top of this, Paul shows us in Colossians 1:18 NIV that Jesus is the *"the firstborn from among the dead."*

This means that Jesus has already blazed a trail for the dead in Christ on the day of the Rapture. Christ was the first to be raised from the dead, the first to have His body transformed and the first to ascend to the sky. Remember our Lord God is always first in everything and the dead in Christ can know that they will soon be resurrected before being taken up to the sky!

Jesus was never the first to be created for God does not create God, and if for some reason you are still struggling about Jesus' status as God the Son, please go to the *"I am"* sayings in the Gospel of John. Every time Jesus said *"I am,"* his Jewish listeners would have understood that He was saying that He is the Messiah.

The sayings include, I am the *"bread of life," "the light of the world,"* the *"gate,"* the *"good shepherd,"* the *"resurrection and the life,"* the *"way and the truth and the life,"* and the *"true vine"* (John 6:35, 8:12, 10:7, 10:11, 11:25, 14:6, 15:1). Though, I have to admit my personal favorite is: *"Before Abraham was, I am (John 8:58 KJV)."*

Every Jew that heard Christ at that point would have understood that Jesus was referring to Himself as God for this is what He said to Moses, *"I AM THAT I AM (Exodus 3:14 KJV)."* Yes, Jesus is the angel of the Lord (Exodus 3:2), who appeared before Moses and is God (Exodus 3:4), and told his prophet that He is the great *"I AM THAT I AM."*

So, returning to apostasy and false prophets, we can but pray for the souls led by movements that deny Christ! We must love them and pray that their spiritual eyes are opened in the same way that we pray for those who are yet to be baptized, the unchurched or those who have forsaken Christ altogether.

Now, let's return to Matthew 24 and the signs! The next one is that *"sin will be rampant (24:12 NLT),"* however, interestingly in NKJV, sin is translated as lawlessness and this is very important. Never have we seen such a collapse in morals in society.

How many videos have you seen of people just walking into a store, taking whatever they want and leaving. No one does anything to stop them. Not even the security teams intervene. They just watch on as shops are pilfered. Consequently, stores close.

Moreover, how often do we see national presidents turning a blind eye to criminals? Just Google lawlessness and you will see the word used daily to describe governments, presidents, towns and cities in Africa, US, Europe and Asia. It is phenomenal.

How many times have local newspapers described London as *"lawless London"* in headlines since the end of the last decade?

We are currently living the warm-up before the Great Tribulation arrives! Why is this happening?

One key factor is that children have stopped praying in schools. Another is that Christ has been banned from public places!

"3 Don't let anyone deceive you in any way, for that day will not come until the rebellion occurs and the man of lawlessness is revealed (2 Thessalonians 2:3)."

We live in a world where good is made to look evil and evil good:

"Woe to those who call evil good
and good evil,
who put darkness for light
and light for darkness,
who put bitter for sweet
and sweet for bitter (Isaiah 5:20 NIV)."

This was not the case at the start of the millennium. Society's position on what is sin or not has changed radically. Human values have shifted dramatically. In the last 20 plus years, everything that was once sinful in the eyes of the courts is no longer punishable in any way whatsoever – abortion is legal or being legalized worldwide, adultery is not a problem anymore, you can just get divorced, it is quick and painless for the adults so that is what matters most to them, pornography is considered healthy by some, adult lewdness and cavorting in front of kindergarten infants is okay, irreversible transgender mutilation of children or adolescents is encouraged and even paid for by different authorities with Christian taxpayer money too.

What is the only sin left standing that is yet to be accepted? The multi-billion-dollar pedophilia industry, but Satan's army is already banging on that door and pushing for acceptance as "children should have the right to control their own sexual lives and follow their own natural inclinations," according to a text, stating the legal position of pedophiles on the US Department of Justice website.

The statement cites how "friendships between older men and boys are viewed as a means of introducing youths to meaningful, emotionally and intellectually fulfilling relationships."

Such relationships are based on pure manipulation, confusion and depravity. I have never known a child, who has said "I want to be abused by an adult."

But I do know of many adults who are scarred for life because they were abused as children. For more, on why some people think pedophilia is a must, check out the text for yourself.

So, what does Peter say about such lawless folk at the end?

"[17] These people are springs without water and mists driven by a storm. Blackest darkness is reserved for them. [18] For they mouth empty, boastful words and, by appealing to the lustful desires of the flesh, they entice people who are just escaping from those who live in error. [19] They promise them freedom, while they themselves are slaves of depravity—for "people are slaves to whatever has mastered them (2 Peter 2:17-19 NIV)."

Moving on from lawlessness, Jesus continues to list more signs including *"the love of most will grow cold (Matthew 24:12 NIV)."* Can you think of a time that people have become more introverted, isolationist, self-serving, chronically stressed and anxious than ever before in the history of the world?

A survey of 90 studies involving 2.2 million adults found that social isolation and feeling lonely respectively lead to a 32% and 14% higher risk of dying early, according to an article published in online monthly journal Nature Human Behaviour.

Publications are calling loneliness either a serious public-health problem or an epidemic. We are social animals – most of us are unable to deal with loneliness, which leads to folk cutting themselves off from others and supposedly protecting themselves by shutting down emotionally.

Consequently, they are sadder and unhealthier. Christians should commune, be in groups. This is how the church started nearly 2,000 years ago in people's homes. Today, however, we are distant, cold. You can see it in congregations where people are asked to hug each other or shake hands or talk to each other and say something simple like "peace be with you."

At such a moment, many are reluctant to interact. So, many Christians are shut down, withdrawn into their own worlds and this is how they like it.

Most would prefer to go to church, put in their 90 minutes of fervor and not have to communicate with anybody whatsoever, before rushing home for Sunday lunch and returning to their lives.

I am thankful that this is not the case at our church because nearly everybody stays for 30 minutes to an hour after Sunday service to mingle, catch up and eat cakes, pastries or other goodies. I am grateful for this closeness, the energy is very different and if someone is feeling shutdown, we usually pray it out of that person before they leave that evening.

You see, while a psychiatrist will be happy to prescribe pills for anxiety, depression, suicidal tendencies and shutdown antisocial behavior, we are quite happy to resolve these issues very quickly through prayer. There is nothing that Jesus cannot do and reverse or heal!

In March 2024, for example, a woman visited us from out of town, however, she had forgotten her antidepressants at home some 407km away. She quickly confessed her problem to me. She needed 150mg of her daily fix to get through her day. I smiled and told her, "I can see your problem, how about we pray it away?"

The Lord showed me a demon on her back. I looked at it. It had been there three years, causing her depression. "In the name of Jesus Christ, I break the power of Satan in the life of Monica (remember how Paul did it in Acts 16:18 NIV?

"In the name of Jesus Christ I command you to come out of her!"), in the name of Jesus Christ, I cast out all malignant influence, oppression…" Before I had finished the sentence, Monica felt a spasm in her lower back and her eyes watered. Lightness came over her and then a smile. The demon had skedaddled! I continued to pray, calling for the Holy Spirit to anoint her in the peace and love of Christ.

"How do you feel?" She was beaming and replied, "I feel light, I feel really light, the depression has gone." This is the power of the mighty name of Jesus Christ combined with the fire of the Holy Spirit!

This is the spiritual authority that the Lord has given to all of us thanks to His name! When moments like this happen the will of the Heavenly Father comes to the fore and the blessings of the future Kingdom of God are revealed in the present!

For Monica, there were no more side-effects. She never went back to the pills and to this day, she remains depression free. And by the next day, she was already speaking in tongues. So depression is spiritual warfare, a form of control, a form of attacking the Lord's people.

In fact, illness is spiritual too! Just a few weeks later, the Lord cured a woman with a herniated disc and sciatic nerve pain. It took seconds for her to be healed in the name of Jesus Christ.

Have you ever had any of these two conditions? I have had depression, herniated discs and sciatic nerve pain - they all hurt. At one point, I had to be rushed to hospital because a herniated disc was so debilitated that I was unable to stand or walk anymore.

If I had met a future version of me back in early 2019 – I would have been healed on the spot in the name of Jesus Christ! Instead, I went through a very invasive surgery, suffered nerve damage, lost sensation in my right leg and spent a month recovering.

Today, I now know that all it takes is faith in Christ and knowing in my heart that Christ wants to heal me by *"His stripes"* on the cross (Isaiah 53:5 NKJV)! So, we are all in a spiritual battle of our lives but in the mighty name of Jesus Christ we can fight temptation, accusation, division, depression, disappointment, dismay, delay, destruction, deception and all of the illnesses you can imagine!

So yes, sadly though, hearts are growing colder because we are losing a spiritual battle that many of us do not even know that we are in! We are oblivious to the truth, and so many of us have walked away from the church and adopted deadly philosophies such as self-righteousness to help us get by on a day-to-day basis.

For so many people worldwide, it seems that the man's or woman's best friend these days is the deeply addictive smartphone and its array of social media channels that allow us to maintain fake and distant social lifestyles and relationships whereby everybody is integrated but in truth completely unintegrated, cold and distant. So what must we do?

We must endure. Cue Matthew 24:13, *"he who endures to the end shall be saved."*

Amid this social destruction, false prophet onslaught, pastors attacking pastors and rebellion in the cities and streets, we must endure to keep the faith in Jesus and be saved! We must endure.

That all said, not all of the signs in Matthew 24 have yet come to pass. For example, the *"gospel of the Kingdom will be preached in all the world as a witness to all the nations, and then the end will come (Matthew 24:14 NIV)."*

This verse speaks to Revival.

We are starting to see some signs of Revival, but we are yet to witness a global wave of preaching of the Kingdom of God that is confirmed with signs and wonders. Though, this is coming!

Another sign that is yet to happen can be found in Matthew 24:27 (NIV), for Christ says: "*For as lightning that comes from the east is visible even in the west, so will be the coming of the Son of Man.*" His comment sheds further light on what the prophet Zechariah wrote in chapter 14:3-9 (NIV):

"[3] Then the LORD will go out and fight against those nations, as he fights on a day of battle. [4] On that day his feet will stand on the Mount of Olives, east of Jerusalem, and the Mount of Olives will be split in two from east to west, forming a great valley, with half of the mountain moving north and half moving south. [5] You will flee by my mountain valley, for it will extend to Azel. You will flee as you fled from the earthquake[a] in the days of Uzziah king of Judah. Then the LORD my God will come, and all the holy ones with him. [6] On that day there will be neither sunlight nor cold, frosty darkness. [7] It will be a unique day—a day known only to the LORD—with no distinction between day and night. When evening comes, there will be light. [8] On that day living water will flow out from Jerusalem, half of it east to the Dead Sea and half of it west to the Mediterranean Sea, in summer and in winter. [9] The LORD will be king over the whole earth. On that day there will be one LORD, and his name the only name."

So those are some of the signs – thankfully not all will come to pass before the Rapture. For example, one of the prophecies is for the planet to be burned to a cinder on the last day – yes, everything will burn up, everything. Now, it would hardly make sense to have a Rapture after the planet has completely melted. Who could survive a heatwave so great that the seas themselves are vaporized? This will not happen to the Lord's people, who will be given a way out thanks to the Rapture. Remember how the Lord spared Noah and Lot and their families? We should be grateful for the Lord's grace and know in our hearts that Christ will make a way for us, for Matthew states as much:

"If those days had not been cut short, no one would survive, but for the sake of the elect those days will be shortened (Matthew 24:22 NIV)."

The Lord will pull us out long before the planet reaches unimaginably hot temperatures (this is not global warming, this is an off-the-scale planetwide cataclysmic event). This will happen on the Day of our Lord (2 Peter 3:10-12). On this final day, the world will be consumed by fire. It will *"come like a thief,"* and will be the climax of the last days prophecies told by the prophets in the Old and New Testaments. Why will this happen? The Lord is wiping the slate clean and paving the way for New Creation but that is a whole other story.

Instead, let's come back to Matthew 24 and ask the following question, why is it so important to know all of these signs? The Lord obviously wants our eyes fixed on Him but He also wants us to be mindful of the End Times prophecies because they will all happen during the same generation, and as before, this generation is called the Noah generation:

""Truly I tell you, this generation will certainly not pass away until all these things have happened (Matthew 24:34 NIV)... [37]As it was in the days of Noah, so it will be at the coming of the Son of Man (24:37 NIV)."

Christ is very clear here about the end. This *"generation will certainly not pass away"* until all of the last days signs are confirmed. Allow me to put this in another way – from the very second that the first of the last days prophecies came to pass, a celestial stopwatch started to count down.

This heavenly clock will only stop when the last prophecy takes place and the world and its final Noah generation are consumed in fire. Again, all of these prophecies will happen during the same generation – the Noah generation.

However, the good news is that Christians, who are in a relationship with Christ, will not see all of the final signs come to pass! For our sake (Matthew 24:22), we will all be raptured first and spared of so much turmoil. How can we know this? Let's look at this verse again:

"If those days had not been cut short, no one would survive, but for the sake of the elect those days will be shortened (Matthew 24:22 NIV)."

The days are cut short not because they are literally shortened as some have supposed but because the Lord is going to take his people before their lives end. He is going to rapture us before our natural time of death. This is the fate of all of the Christians who are in a relationship with Christ. Their days will be shortened because they will be raptured and spared the horrors of the Great Tribulation.

So, there you have it. The clues are laid bare. The Rapture is one of the many End Times signs that will happen during the same generation, otherwise known as the Noah generation. I will keep repeating this because it is an important point.

According to Christ, this Noah generation exists twice in the history of humanity and in both cases only the righteous survived (Noah and his family) and will survive (believers in a relationship with Christ) in the future! So what more can we learn about this Noah generation? Christ provides more insight:

"38 For in the days before the flood, people were eating and drinking, marrying and giving in marriage, up to the day Noah entered the ark; 39 and they knew nothing about what would happen until the flood came and took them all away. That is how it will be at the coming of the Son of Man (Matthew 24:38-39 NIV)."

This particular verse haunted me one evening during the pandemic as I drove with my wife to dinner and we passed one of the trendiest streets in São Paulo.

With a sense of loss, I watched from the car as folk thronged around the outdoor bars and queued for a much-sought-after place in one of the many contemporary restaurants on *Rua Jerônimo da Veiga.*

The clientele looked oblivious and brimming over with their many self-interests of that evening, living a life of pleasure-chasing overload.

As I looked at this road, I imagined this is what Jesus meant by "*they knew nothing about what would happen until the flood came and took them away.*" History is repeating itself. We are part of this Noah generation prophesied by Christ!

In short, the people of Earth will be unaware of Jesus' coming back just like they were unaware of the great flood in Genesis 7:23 when *"He destroyed all living things which were on the face of the ground: both man and cattle, creeping thing and bird of the air. They were destroyed from the earth. Only Noah and those who were with him in the ark remained alive (NKJV)."*

The violent and corrupt people of the first Noah generation were caught out because "*on that day all the springs of the great deep burst forth, and the floodgates of the heavens were opened (Genesis 7:11 NIV)."* There was no way out as the water came from the ground and the sky, and so it will be with the Rapture, the Great Tribulation and the second coming of Christ.

Let's return to Matthew 24 to understand this no way-out scenario better. Immediately after Jesus talks about the Noah generation in verse 39, Christ then focuses on the Rapture.

"[40] *Two men will be in the field; one will be taken and the other left.* [41] *Two women will be grinding with a hand mill; one will be taken and the other left."*

The Rapture is going to happen no matter what. There is no way out for those who are in a relationship with Christ, for they will go, and for those who are not, they will stay. For the Lord needs to take us before the Great Tribulation. The rule of the antichrist is coming – nothing can change that either.

Thankfully the Rapture is coming to pull us out before the worst of the signs in Matthew 24 and Revelation happen. And glorious will be that day, the Rapture day, glorious for the Lord and for the dead and living who go in Christ! Amen?

However, are you still in doubt? Have you been convinced? What is the Holy Spirit telling you? If no, what more can we learn about the end before the Rapture? What more can we learn about the Noah generation?

And what else must we know about the Rapture itself? Fortunately, Matthew was not the only one who was with Jesus when He gave his Olivet Discourse. Peter was also there and he has a different take to Matthew that allows us to learn more about what our Lord God is planning for all of us until the Rapture – the last day of the Church on earth!

Let's investigate this further and look at 2 Peter 2. In this text, Peter writes that the Lord protected Noah, *"a preacher of righteousness, and seven others (2 Peter 2:5 NIV),"* when he destroyed the *"ancient world."* Peter also wrote that the Lord *"rescued Lot, a righteous man, who was distressed by the depraved conducts of the lawless (2 Peter 2:7 NIV)."* Is there a comparison here between Noah or Lot or is Peter instead making the same point?

Well, it is very clear that the Lord protects the righteous. We also see that it is Noah's and Lot's relationship, faith and trust in the Lord God that saved them. This is a huge deal and is a great cause for hope! Why?

Peter's take on Noah and Lot is that our Lord God is going to give us a way out at some point so that we are not going to be there on the day when the world is burned to a cinder as prophesied by Peter in 2 Peter 3. We will not have to fear for our lives on that day for we will have already been saved – we will already have been raptured. The Lord will spare us of that terrible cataclysmic earth-shattering day.

We can safely conclude that the Rapture will be one massive global airlift of unimaginable proportions over the course of a mere 100 to 150 milliseconds.

For the Lord *"knows how to rescue the godly from trials (2 Peter 2:9 NIV)."* The Rapture is a way out for all of our Lord God's children, and by children, I mean those who are in a relationship in Christ, those who have faith in Christ and are reborn in Him (John 1:12).

I cannot reiterate this point enough. Relationship is key here. For only those who are born again can see the Kingdom of God (John 3:3) and will be saved on the day of the Rapture – there is no wiggle room, or loopholes to secure a place up in the sky!

Unlike Noah's time, however, the world will not be flooded.

Instead it will be burned to a cinder when *"the heavens will disappear with a roar; the elements will be destroyed by fire, and the earth and everything done in it will be laid bare (2 Peter 3:10 NIV)."*

Everything is going to be toast, fortunately as was established earlier in this chapter, those who are saved during the Rapture will never have to experience the anguish of dying in such a terrible way on that day when "*the elements will melt in the heat (2 Peter 3:12 NIV).*"

That all said, is there enough proof to say that we really are part of the Noah generation? Well, societal decline is glaringly obvious – moral values have never been so devalued. This is clearly exacerbated by governments banning prayer in schools and removing scriptures as a subject from school syllabuses. But are we not going in circles at this stage? Really? What else can we know?

To understand that we are at the end and to be sure we are part of the Noah generation, we need to remember what Christ said during the Olivet Discourse. Let's go back to Matthew 24:34 and look at it with a fresh lens: *"Truly I tell you, this generation will certainly not pass away until all these things have happened."*

As before, Christ is stating that all of the End Times prophecies will happen during the same generation and that that generation will not die until all of the prophecies have happened during the same period of up to 100 years. Right?

So, the question to ask now is when did these End Times prophecies start because so many have either come to pass or are being fulfilled or are glaringly on the horizon. This is when we need to look at other End Times prophecies in the Bible. Cue Isaiah 66:8 (TLB):

"For in one day, suddenly, a nation, Israel, shall be born, even before the birth pains comes. In a moment, just as Israel's anguish starts, the baby is born; the nation begins."

Isaiah prophesied between 700-681 BC that Israel would be born again in just one day. This prophetic verse in Isaiah was fulfilled May 14, 1948. Israel was reborn with the Declaration of the Establishment of the State of Israel. How was it possible for Israel to be reestablished in just one day?

Well, the process of the nation's rebirth took decades of work ahead of May 14, 1948. The Lord used the British Empire during its height and decline to bring about Israel. Key moments include British Foreign Secretary Arthur Balfour expressing government support for a Jewish homeland in a letter to Baron Lionel Rothschild in late 1917.

This came just years before Winston Churchill, the Secretary of State for the Colonies, visited Jerusalem, Gaza and Cairo in 1921, and after receiving Emir Abdullah, Transjordan became an Arab kingdom under Abdullah that same year, while it was determined that western Palestine from the Mediterranean to the Jordan River would be ruled by Britain with a commitment to continued Jewish immigration – in line with then British government policy.

Of course, this is an oversimplification of what happened then as numerous agreements were made at the League of Nations that established different states post the Franco-Syrian war of 1920 and the break-up of the Ottoman Empire.

Ultimately, it would take another book to list the many events that contributed to the rebirth of Israel in one day, but it is important to note Churchill's critical role in supporting the reestablishment of the Zionist state, leading to Israel's declaration of independence in 1948.

For in "one day" Israel was reborn before the birth pains happened, according to Isaiah. Where do we also see the birth pains mentioned? You have guessed it, Matthew 24, where Christ said:

"'Watch out that no one deceives you. [5] For many will come in my name, claiming, 'I am the Messiah,' and will deceive many. [6] You will hear of wars and rumors of wars, but see to it that you are not alarmed. Such things must happen, but the end is still to come. [7] Nation will rise against nation, and kingdom against kingdom. There will be famines and earthquakes in various places. [8] All these are the beginning of birth pains (Matthew 24:4-8 NIV)."

Christ says above that wars and rumors of war, nation against nation, famines and earthquakes are just the beginning of the birth pains. What comes after the start to birth pains includes

Christian persecution and believers being *"hated by all nations"*, with many turning *"away from the faith,"* while betraying and hating each other (Matthew 24:9), and so on.

In other words, Israel's independence came in 1948 before the birth pains. And all of the wars after the reestablishment of Israel represent the start to the birth pains. It is safe to conclude that we are now living in a world that has already witnessed the start to the birth pains listed in Matthew 24 and that the end itself will come when the Gospel of the Kingdom is preached in the whole world (Matthew 24:14).

So, what do we know at this point? We are the Noah generation. We also know that the world has already witnessed the signs before the birth pains, the signs at the start of the birth pains and the signs after the beginning of the birth pains. The question now is when did this Noah generation start?

Here is the thing, we cannot answer this question by looking at Isaiah or Matthew alone. We need to go further afield and try to pinpoint this further. Indeed, what more can the Bible tell us? Psalm 102 is a harrowing account of the Holocaust during World War II, for example:

"For my days vanish like smoke;
my bones burn like glowing embers.
4 *My heart is blighted and withered like grass;*
I forget to eat my food.
5 *In my distress I groan aloud*
and am reduced to skin and bones.
6 *I am like a desert owl,*
like an owl among the ruins.
7 *I lie awake; I have become*
like a bird alone on a roof.
8 *All day long my enemies taunt me;*
those who rail against me use my name as a curse.
9 *For I eat ashes as my food*
and mingle my drink with tears
10 *because of your great wrath,*
for you have taken me up and thrown me aside.

[11] My days are like the evening shadow;
I wither away like grass (Psalm 102:3-11 NIV)."

Meanwhile, Ezekiel 37 speaks to the resulting horror of the Holocaust (v1-2) and what the Lord will do with His people afterward (v21b-22):

"[1] The hand of the LORD was on me, and he brought me out by the Spirit of the LORD and set me in the middle of a valley; it was full of bones. [2] He led me back and forth among them, and I saw a great many bones on the floor of the valley, bones that were very dry... [21b] I will gather them from all around and bring them back into their own land. [22] I will make them one nation in the land, on the mountains of Israel. There will be one king over all of them and they will never again be two nations or be divided into two kingdoms (Ezekiel 37:1-2, 21b-22 NIV.)

You can see in verses 21b to 22 in Ezekiel that they speak to the reestablishment of the Israeli state. Meanwhile, Esther 9:12-14 prophesies the hangings of the 10 in the wake of the Nuremberg trials in 1946. The 10 should have died by firing squad or been put in an electric chair in line with US legislation, but no, they were hanged instead.

"[12] And the king said to Queen Esther, "In Susa the citadel the Jews have killed and destroyed 500 men and also the ten sons of Haman. What then have they done in the rest of the king's provinces! Now what is your wish? It shall be granted you. And what further is your request? It shall be fulfilled." [13] And Esther said, "If it please the king, let the Jews who are in Susa be allowed tomorrow also to do according to this day's edict. And let the ten sons of Haman be hanged on the gallows." [14] So the king commanded this to be done. A decree was issued in Susa, and the ten sons of Haman were hanged (Esther 9:12-14 ESV)."

This is interesting, we are clearly connecting prophecies in the Old Testament with world history in the 1940s and this takes us back to the reestablishment of Israel in one day in 1948. Again, there are more examples in Jeremiah and Hosea as so many prophecies in other Old and New Testament books have come to pass. However, to detail them would require the writing of another book.

In summary, so many signs are under way since World War II and Israel became a nation again, and if that is not enough to convince folk that we are at the end – allow me to add another telltale sign that ties us to the Noah generation.

We need only look to the current war between Hamas and Israel that started October 7, 2023, and continues in 2024. Hamas is the Hebrew word for violence (חָמָֽס׃). Hamas also appears in the Hebrew text of Genesis at the end of Genesis 6:11 NIV: *"Now the earth was corrupt in God's sight and was full of violence."* Why is this verse so relevant? This verse comes just three verses after the words: "*This is the account of Noah and his family (Genesis 6:9 NIV).*"

Please dear reader do not say in your mind, "oh look at that, what a coincidence." There are no coincidences in the Bible. Symbols, names, colors, smells, context, historical symmetries and repetitions, visions, dreams and much more are all part of His design for us.

Everything is used for the good purpose of the Lord's ministry of the church, His servants and people. The use of the Hebrew word for violence in Genesis 6:11 is just one more glaring marker for us to help us know in our hearts and minds that the world's population is inextricably linked to the Noah generation and that the end is coming.

Ultimately, the timing of all of this is very important because Jesus says in Matthew 24 that all of the End Times signs will happen during the course of one generation, and as we already know this generation is the Noah generation, and one generation lasts 100 years in the Bible.

So if, we look to the Old Testament prophecies that speak to the horrors of World War II, the reestablishment of the state of Israel that came before the birth pains, the signs that have since been fulfilled such as wars and rumors of wars at the start of the birth pains, and then we note that we are in the throes of the Great Apostasy in the wake of the 21st century digital age, we could be some 85 years into the Noah generation, or almost at the end of the 100-year generation period, if we use 1939 (the start of the Second World War II) as our initial marker. If we do that and subtract 2024 from 1939, you have 85 years.

Could it be that we have just 15 years and change left for the Noah generation to end? Or is there more time? Did Jesus want us to subtract from a marker at the start of the birth pains (post the reestablishment of the Israeli state) and not before the birth pains began?

In other words, did the Noah generation only begin after Israel was reestablished when there were wars and rumors of wars? Should we then start with the North Korean war or Vietnam as potential markers? Jesus did not list all of the End Times prophecies during the Olivet Discourse.

He gave examples – key pointers in fact – so that we not only look to Matthew 24 and other texts in the Gospels but also to other End Times prophecies in the Old Testament.

Now, it is important to note that so many brighter theologians and pastors have already tried to predict the end and failed. However, I am not trying to calculate when the end will come.

The goal of this book is to warn Christians and prepare them for the Rapture, to show them what to expect, what it means and what the Lord wants us to do in the final years. For the Lord has put this into my heart – otherwise I would not have written this book.

However, it is important to contextualize, pinpoint and eliminate all possibilities. So, reverting to the vision and bearing in mind what we know of the End Times prophecies and that we are part of the Noah generation, we must remember that my father, who was born in 1946, came a little before the birth pains began and he is evidence in my vision from the Lord that the Rapture will come during his lifetime and mine.

So let's recap! All of the End Times prophecies will happen during the same generation and that is called the Noah generation, which happens twice in the history of the world. The End Times prophecies started at the very least during World War II.

The reestablishment of Israel is a key End Times sign. And whether we have 10 years, 15, 20 or a little more than that left before the Rapture happens, we can know from the vision that it will take place during the lifetime of my father.

You see, if dad had not appeared in the vision, I might not have written this book and would have simply concluded that the Rapture would likely happen at some point in my lifetime instead - perhaps sometime in the next 50 years.

Instead, the Lord – in His infinite wisdom – has given me a keen sense of urgency about the situation, and rightly so by placing my 77-year-old dad in the vision. Consequently, I am keenly aware that time is running out as the signs around the world continue to be confirmed.

Lastly, and as before, I cannot tell you when the Rapture will happen – the Lord did not provide any more clues and pointers beyond those in the Bible and the dream of the Rapture itself, which will take place in my future church office in England.

Please note dear reader that I did not physically see my father in the vision as we were talking over the phone, so I am unable to identify or estimate his final age on the day of the Rapture. And as before, this book is focused on breaking down the last minute before the Rapture, what we can expect once we are in the sky and how we should live these final years and prepare.

For the Lord has shown me all of these things and we can be sure that for the sake of the elect, the Lord's timing will be perfect on that rapturous day when He will airlift us out just in time! For that is the purpose of the Rapture – to rescue His people and spare us all of the Great Tribulation - just like He did with Noah and His ark of salvation! And on that day, the glory will be the Lord's and no one else's (Isaiah 42:8) thanks to the power of the Holy Spirit's Fire of God.

Lastly, while I am not keen to give my opinion here because we must be wary of anyone who says the Rapture is in such and such year, and that Jesus will come back in such and such year and that the day of our Lord will be in such and such month or year, I would recommend that everybody keeps their eyes peeled in the coming years.

Why? As I write this text on Sunday morning February 25, 2024, I am in Brazil. I am quietly anxious for this evening's service and what the Lord will do this day at church, however, I am fully conscious of the fact that I was raptured in my future church office somewhere in England.

The vision of the Rapture points to my ministry ending in Europe and I already know in my heart that I will be moving back home soon – for the Lord has told me as much. So if we are indeed at the end, and we are, then the antichrist cannot be far off either! Is this really it then, is the antichrist really among us and the world is being prepared to worship him? And where does that leave humanity?

Chapter 7
The antichrist is here, what should we do?

"But the Lord is faithful, and he will strengthen and protect you from the evil one (2 Thessalonians 3:3 NIV)."

It goes without saying that if we are indeed at the end, that the Rapture is to come, that Jesus is to return, then it becomes apparent that the prophesied antichrist cannot be far away. Now, this is an obvious deduction if we think about it but it was not obvious to me.

In fact, I was so rushed with every other detail of the vision itself, meditating on it, analyzing, praying and weighing up the Bible verses that emerged that it had not remotely occurred to me to look at the bigger picture, take a step back and better examine what this would mean to the world in the last days.

I was still coming to grips with the vision itself – and continuously asking questions such as is this dream for real, is this from the Lord, did my subconscious imagine it, am I going nuts and is this really the end?

It was not until I was on holiday with my family at the beach at the end of July 2023 – nearly six weeks after the vision, that the Holy Spirit popped the following thought into my mind, "*the antichrist is here.*" My initial reaction was to kick myself, "of course, why on earth didn't I think of that?" I suddenly had a very dim view about my deductive reasoning.

Here I was contemplating the end and the antichrist had never occurred to me. I confess this. If the subject were not so serious, it would have been comic at just how obvious this point was and continues to be.

I then briefly imagined what the world could be like once the antichrist takes power, subduing all nations and tribes worldwide as prophesied in Revelation.

As I contemplated such a bleak reality, I wrote down the words "*the antichrist is here.*" I did not want to forget such valuable information ahead of a service that I was set to give about the Rapture in August.

Incredibly, though, and despite all efforts to remember, I did forget about the antichrist. I had a lot on my mind as I daily meditated and prayed on how to best deliver a service about the Rapture.

You see, at this point, three of four pastors had already confirmed the veracity of the dream, however, there were still questions that needed to be answered. This came as the Lord also continued to reveal something new about the vision on a daily basis. I was a sponge collecting lots of information from the Bible, while praying and meditating on the Rapture.

You see it was easy for me to forget about the antichrist. I was far more concerned about preparing for the upcoming service. Just two days before I was headed for the pulpit, the Holy Spirit, who is my guide, teacher, trainer, confidant and most intimate friend who knows of all of my thoughts, reminded me again of the antichrist. How?

As I opened the Bible that Friday morning, God the Spirit gave me this verse:

"But the Lord is faithful, and he will strengthen and protect you from the evil one (2 Thessalonians 3:3 NIV)."

As my eyes landed on the words "*evil one*," I suddenly remembered what the Holy Spirit had told me on the beach. I chided myself for forgetting about the antichrist as I started to mull over the implications of such a presence in the world.

Who forgets that kind of information after all, really? As I contemplated 2 Thessalonians 3:3, the following verses sprang to mind, *"fix your thoughts on Jesus (Hebrews 3:1 NIV),"* and *"seek the Kingdom of God above all else and live righteously, and He will give you everything you need (Matthew 6:33 NLT)."*

The Holy Spirit was reminding me that what matters most is Jesus Christ and that we must fix our eyes and thoughts on our Lord – no matter what the circumstance or scenario, especially when we walk through the darkest valley.

This is what the Holy Spirit does – He guides us back to Christ and reveals His glory so that we can know in our hearts and minds that He is our Lord God, and that with Him we are saved, healed, protected, blessed and prospered.

By fixing our eyes on Christ, we become more like Him, for we are made in our Lord God's image, and we are called to be imitators of Christ.

For the second we accept Jesus, we become perfect but we spend the rest of our lives being made holy through the care and direction of the Holy Spirit (Hebrews 10:14).

This is why Paul underscores the importance of living in God the Spirit (Romans 8:1-9) and not in our fleshy ways. It is all a process of surrendering to the Lord that involves the mortification of our carnal lifestyles, however, none of this transformation is possible without the Holy Spirit.

One cannot change oneself and remain changed – but the Holy Spirit can! And as we develop, grow, mature, we end up asking ourselves a key question – *"who am I in Christ?"*

When we contemplate our true identity in the Lord, where we have come from and what Christ has done in our lives, with time, our perception and image of who we are gradually transform.

We come to understand our responsibilities in Christ as a spouse, parent, colleague or leader in the lives of others. In short, we change and so does the way we understand and read the Bible.

For we all have a role in the Kingdom of God. This is extremely powerful when we seek Christ to know Him for who He is in our lives and what He has done. Really, the more we do this the more we end up seeing His hand in everything. When we understand His love, care and purpose in our life, we see Christ in a new light and eventually, we come to know Him.

So this is the first message that I received from the Lord, to fix our eyes on the Lord. The second, "*seek the Kingdom of God above all else and live righteously, and He will give you everything you need (Matthew 6:33 NLT),*" is a way of life. Indeed, how do you start your day? Do you pick up a cellphone or do you renew your faith in Christ? Do you go to WhatsApp, Instagram or email or do you confess and pray to start the day?

The Lord expects us to put Him first, not second and certainly not 20th on our list of to dos before heading out to work or school. Waking up five minutes earlier to pray is a small but important first step to seeking the Lord at the start of the day. We need to give thanks for so many blessings in our lives. We would not be here if it were not by His authority.

The existence we have, the oxygen we breathe, the hairs on our head (or not) are all by His authority and permission.

Seeking God first when we wake up matters – even if it is only to say thank you. Indeed, if we have a devotional or a Bible in One Year to read and meditate on before leaving our bed, we are setting ourselves up for the day. Spiritual bread in the morning helps us to deal with the stress that inevitably ensues. If you do this long enough, one day, stress passes as you migrate to a God-dependent lifestyle and that is a whole other ballgame.

Okay, let's return to 2 Thessalonians 3:3 NIV and the antichrist: *"But the Lord is faithful, and he will strengthen and protect you from the evil one."*

Now, let's look at this verse in light of the Rapture. There is a promise here and that is that the Lord will *"strengthen"* and *"protect"* us. Indeed, as the days darken and the world is prepared to worship the antichrist, the Lord will strengthen us so that we can endure to the end!

This is why it is important to fix our eyes on Christ and seek Him at the start of our day to set us up for the inevitable trials that come. But what about the protection? Well, there are two moments here. The Lord will take care of us and be there when we need Him, protecting us on a day-to-day basis. But there is more.

Remember that the purpose of the Rapture is to rescue us? What are we being rescued from? The Great Tribulation, but why will this extremely bleak moment in the history of the world be so grim? Simple – the antichrist and the darkness that he is planning for the world.

So, the purpose of the Rapture is not just to rescue us, it is to protect us and that is the aim of this great day. For His glory, Christ is going to airlift billions through the power of the Holy Spirit and save us from the horrors of the upcoming tribulation because our Lord is not only bound by the promise made in 2 Thessalonians 3:3 but by His New Covenant in all of us. Hang on, wait a minute, where on earth does it say that?

Cue the Lord's prayer: *"Lead us not into temptation but deliver us from the evil one (Matthew 6:13 NLT)?"* You see, the basic premise of the covenant is that Christ has our back from the moment we wake up until the moment we sleep at the end of the day. For our enemies become His enemies and vice-versa.

This is why the Lord gives us the tools to protect ourselves, *"For the weapons of our warfare are not carnal but mighty in God for pulling down strongholds (2 Corinthians 10:4 NIV)."*

What is such a weapon? Tis the mighty name of the Lord Jesus Christ – for the devil's henchmen must obey His name, which is given to us to defend ourselves from the enemy whenever we see fit. How come? Well, the Heavenly Father gave Jesus control and authority over heaven, earth, death and hell (Revelation 1:18, Matthew 28:18).

In the name of Jesus, we can heal, we can cast out evil spirits, prophesy and so much more! So what is the action required of us? We just have to ask the Lord and with time, if not immediately, we will receive the supernatural gifts from the Holy Spirit for the benefit of the Kingdom of God.

On top of that, we have prayer. So, do you pray daily and ask for total protection in the name of Jesus Christ? Please do, the benefits are so many because when you do, you are exercising faith and demonstrating trust in Him as well as gaining protection – sometimes in ways you will never ever know about or possibly expect!

So, the Rapture is nothing less than the climax to the promise made in 2 Thessalonians 3:3. That said, there is also a historical context to the verse: *"But the Lord is faithful, and he will strengthen and protect you from the evil one."* It is important to note that when Paul wrote to the Thessalonians there was an expectation among first century believers in Christ that Jesus was coming back in their lifetimes and that the Rapture would also happen.

The verse in 2 Thessalonians 3:3 had an immediate practical aspect to the readers of that epistle in either AD 51 or AD 52 when the apostle first wrote it. Consequently, the verses in 2 Thessalonians 3:3, or rather 2 Thessalonians 3:1-3, have served as an inspiration for all Christians ever since the first century. This is important for we are all under demonic oppression of some kind and have battles to fight.

Another key word in 2 Thessalonians 3:3 is faithful. This is really important. Why? Faithful means that Jesus' position does not change, for He is the same yesterday, today and tomorrow.

That means, and as before within the context of the New Covenant, the Lord has our backs.

We can expect Christ to be there for us. He is not going to abandon us, for He is faithful. By working alongside the Holy Spirit, whose depth of patience is beyond our understanding and our own very limited reserves of patience, Jesus will help us work through the challenges as they arise.

And how does that all work? Relationship. We all need relationship in Jesus Christ before the Rapture so our minds are being renewed and our hearts are being transformed by Him. Through Him, we also receive wisdom – and an ability to see through the enemy's lies and deceptions in our lives.

Again, the message is clear. Fix your eyes and thoughts on Jesus Christ. Consequently, the new verse, *"But the Lord is faithful, and he will strengthen and protect you from the evil one (2 Thessalonians 3:3 NIV),"* was inserted into my presentation just two days before the August 13 service. I kept repeating in my mind, wow, wow, wow, the antichrist is here. I felt like a school kid again as if the information the Lord had just provided me with (again) was like that of a new toy being put into my hands. I marveled at the possibilities of what it meant.

So, let's recap! We must remember to fix our eyes and thoughts on Jesus Christ, putting the Lord's will above our own desires and knowing in our hearts that relationship matters most for He has our backs and is protecting us until the day of the Rapture.

For the purpose of the Rapture is to rescue us so we are protected from the Great Tribulation. However, that is not all. If our eyes and thoughts are fixed on Christ, how should we live until the Rapture comes? How can we acquit ourselves admirably before the Lord on that Judgement Day when He will ask us, *"so what did you do with the talents and gifts that I gave you? Did you help others? How did you apply My Word to your life?"*

Chapter 8
Planning for the journey and living a life worth living

"If you are wise and understand God's ways, prove it by living an honorable life, doing good works with the humility that comes from wisdom (James 3:13 NLT)."

If a doctor were to say to you today that you have just 10 years to live, what would you do? Would you care, freak out, or make a bucket list? Or would you feel a tug on your heart? Would you feel a pricking of the conscience? Would you reconsider your life choices? Now, what would happen if Jesus were to the say the same? And what if you knew that every person on the planet faces what is called Judgment Day and on that day we will have to give account to the Lord of what we have done in our lives?

For we will all have to *"appear before the judgment seat of Christ, so that each of us may receive what is due us for the things done while in the body, whether good or bad (2 Corinthians 5:10 NIV)."*

How should we live with the knowledge that the Rapture is coming? Is this not the same as asking ourselves, how should we best lead a Christian life? Perhaps, we need to rethink our values? Indeed, what is a life worth living? Have you asked what our Lord would want for you and from you?

Perhaps this could finally be a good time to start thinking about those big life changes that have been put off time and time again. Such changes would go deeper than a mere analysis of how we behave or how we treat others – though both points are important.

The clock is ticking, time is really finite, it is really running out and there is a greater sense of urgency about the matter than ever before. Again, imagine, Jesus is right in front of you with His arm extended forward and hand open inviting you to take action.

Will you like so many just do nothing or will you ask the question, "how can I have the biggest impact on others in the shortest time possible before it runs out in God's one-day sand clock? What will be my legacy in Christ, how can I serve others?"

These are some of the questions that I asked myself after the Lord had shown me that the antichrist is already among us. I said to the Lord, how can we live in an age like this, how can we prepare for the end? This is the verse the Lord gave;

"If you are wise and understand God's ways, prove it by living an honorable life, doing good works with the humility that comes from wisdom (James 3:13 NLT)."

So, there you have it! Our Lord God wants everybody who is wise and understanding in His ways to serve. For me at least, alea jacta est, the die is cast! It is clear that we have all crossed the Rubicon, we have passed the point of no return! Again, Matthew 24:38 NIV springs to mind!

For Christ said it will be like the *"days before the flood, people were eating and drinking, marrying and giving in marriage, up to the day Noah entered the ark;* [39] *and they knew nothing about what would happen until the flood came and took them all away."*

How this verse weighs on my heart. This cannot be a time for us to just sit around, binge on the next season of the Crown on Netflix, gorge on goodies and live a life of digital distraction until the next dopamine fix. Surely not! This is also not a time for us to be isolated, while waiting for the Fire of God to come down from the sky and rescue us from a world that we no longer wish to be part of. This is not what our Lord wants either.

Yes, He wants us to be in a relationship but Christ needs us to all get involved and tell others about His return so that Christendom worldwide is prepared. This is the time and the time is now, for the Lord is challenging us, daring us, willing us to step outside of our comfort zone and serve, and not in any old way, but to serve with the type of humility that comes from His wisdom.

Indeed, our Lord wants us to acquit ourselves in style and in the most Christlike fashion possible! James 3:13 is deeply profound and it speaks volumes about how we should live, however, we need to understand its broader context before we can grasp its true depth – for how deep can wisdom truly go after all?

Before grappling with the verse further, it is important to note that the Lord has singled out only one verse in James' letter. This is no ordinary epistle. In fact, I love it and it is written by Christ's brother, who was leader of the church in Jerusalem.

Why is it so special? James focused on right Christian behavior, religious hypocrisy and the challenges of daily living. He also examined correct worship and exposed the worst thing about all of us – our tongue and how it can damage relationships and people's lives.

Interestingly, James, who was not a disciple but came to Christ after His resurrection, calls on Christians to have faith and trust in Jesus, for the Lord will help us through hard times. Indeed, how can we endure in the face of so many challenges? James cites Job's perseverance as an example:

"[11] As you know, we count as blessed those who have persevered. You have heard of Job's perseverance and have seen what the Lord finally brought about. The Lord is full of compassion and mercy (James 5:11 NIV)."

He reminds readers that prayer of a righteous person is powerful and effective (James 5:16-18) and that patience, standing firm and not complaining are paramount:

"[8] You too, be patient and stand firm, because the Lord's coming is near. [9] Don't grumble against one another, brothers and sisters, or you will be judged. The Judge is standing at the door! (James 5:8-9 NIV)."

In summary, James' letter is a highly practical guide to a life worth living, highlighting that we can be confident that our faith will be rewarded when Christ returns and yes, we should be patient until then. James moves back and forth between these themes throughout his epistle, telling believers to be doers of the Word. Here is one of his commands to action:

"Do not merely listen to the word, and so deceive yourselves. Do what it says (James 1:22 NIV)."

So, this takes us back to James 3:13 and the Lord's rousing call for us to reach out, tell others about Christ and give testimony wherever we are – albeit in our homes, office, streets, cinema, store or church.

"If you are wise and understand God's ways, prove it by living an honorable life, doing good works with the humility that comes from wisdom (James 3:13 NLT)."

Why is this so rousing? Do you know what it is like to be suddenly connected to a stranger on a street because the Lord revealed to you the deepest secrets to his or her life, and you are suddenly filled with compassion for that soul?

For a moment, that person's problems become your own, and you find yourself praying and pleading to the Lord on so many levels. Why?

People often need deliverance from pain, bitterness, addiction, jealousy, hatred, unforgiveness, envy or spiritual apathy. Sometimes, they need healing too.

Typically, they suffer from a chronic illness that science cannot resolve, and if they have faith, they are healed. The Lord does not disappoint for He reveals much during prayer. On top of this, there are those who are called to ministry.

How often this comes to light during prayer! The reactions are diverse. Some have no idea that they had a ministerial calling and are little moved by the revelation.

If anything, it causes consternation because they already lead such busy lives. There are those who jump up and down with delight because they have long wanted to serve. Meanwhile, there are others, who know they have such a calling but are not yet ready to embrace it.

And we cannot forget the few who are baptized in the Holy Spirit and fire, and receive the supernatural gifts of the Holy Spirit. Whoosh.

Most tear up at that point as the Lord reveals that He is giving them the gifts of speaking in tongues, prophecy, revelation and healing, for example. Why?

Such souls typically have a calling to evangelize, to bring others to Christ.

Indeed, within a few minutes of prayer, a person's life could change and be set on a completely different course as it becomes blatantly clear that Christ is very busy, present and involved in the lives of all of His children.

Oh, and don't even get me started when someone is about to come to Christ for the first time and you can see the Lord opening his or her spiritual eyes as that person is convicted of sins and accepts Jesus as Lord and Savior.

The Holy Spirit not only pours on me His joy but confirms to me that a party is under way in heaven at that very moment because a sinner repented! Awesome, right but is that it? No!

Years of depression are wiped out in seconds by the power of the Holy Spirit. Panic attacks, anxiety and suicidal thoughts are all gone! Rousing? It is AWESOME, it is the Kingdom of God being revealed in the 21st century and the Lord wants an army of servants to do this worldwide.

Awesome is the only word that comes to mind at a moment like this. Indeed, awesome is not for a football game or a cookie or a video game, awesome should only be used to describe who our Lord God is and what He does, for I am in awe of His awesome deeds!

So let's head back to James 3:13, the verse the Lord gave on how we should live until the Rapture itself happens! Let's recap here and break it down:

"If you are wise and understand God's ways, prove it by living an honorable life, doing good works with the humility that comes from wisdom (James 3:13 NLT)."

Firstly, if we are to live the way the Lord wants us to live, we must be wise and understand God's ways. This means being wise is a requirement here. But what does that mean to be wise?

Have you ever felt particularly wise? Do you know what it means to be wise according to the Lord, or wise in the eyes of men? Is there a difference? And here is the thing, do you feel wise? There is a trap here, read on:

"The way of a fool is right in his own eyes, but a wise man listens to advice (Proverbs 12:15 ESV)."

That is not exactly encouraging. And what about human wisdom? Paul puts it into perspective, *"For the foolishness of God is wiser than human wisdom, and the weakness of God is stronger than human strength (1 Corinthians 1:25 NIV)."* Paul goes further, *"for the wisdom of the world is foolishness with God. As the Scriptures say, 'He traps the wise in the snare of their own cleverness (1 Corinthians 3:19 NLT)."*

How many times have we read about the Pharisees trying to trick Jesus with their clever questions? They always failed miserably.

So how can we possibly be wise? James has the answer, *"if you need wisdom, ask our generous God, and he will give it to you. He will not rebuke you for asking (James 1:5 NIV)."* Indeed, wisdom, knowledge and understanding come from the Lord (Proverbs 2:6) and the beginning of wisdom is to get wisdom (Proverbs 4:7) and there are clear benefits for the *"one who gets wisdom loves life; the one who cherishes understanding will soon prosper (Proverbs 19:8 NIV)."*

When we obtain wisdom, we realize that real wisdom starts with the fear of our Lord for, "*the fear of the Lord is the beginning of knowledge but fools despise wisdom and instruction, Proverbs 1:7 NIV).*" The next step is to grow in wisdom to help us succeed in life by trusting the Lord, listening to advice, and delighting in His discipline, (Proverbs 22:17, 29:11, Proverbs 3:11-12, Hebrews 12:5).

For many, orderliness or understanding the essence of life is wisdom but to obtain the Lord's wisdom is to take the following command to heart and allow the Holy Spirit to do the rest:

"Therefore be imitators of God as dear children. 2 And walk in love, as Christ also has loved us and given Himself for us, an offering and a sacrifice to God for a sweet-smelling aroma (Ephesians 5:1 NKJV)."

Wisdom will come naturally as we seek the Lord and move closer to Him. The fruits of the Spirit will be conceded and with time we too will reflect His love, joy, peace, patience, kindness, goodness, faithfulness, gentleness and self-control, so that others can also see more of Christ in us and less of us in us! He increases while we decrease.

For when we ask for wisdom, the Lord will grant us what we ask because we are making a Christlike request. In such a situation, our Heavenly Father holds nothing back. If the person's heart is in the right place, the Lord will gladly agree to such a wish. He will not deny His children something that is in His nature and of His nature. Would not a father delight in his child seeking greater wisdom and understanding? Who would deny such a request?

For wisdom is *"first of all pure… peace loving, gentle at all times, and willing to yield to others (3:17 NLT)."* Does this not sound familiar? James is clearly describing the example that Jesus left. And like Christ, we must also be *"peacemakers"* who *"will plant seeds of* peace *and reap a harvest of righteousness (v18 NLT)"* in our lives. However, we must also be wary of the pitfalls and risks of allowing evil thoughts to fester in our hearts and minds as we seek to grow in Christ:

"But if you are bitterly jealous and there is selfish ambition in your heart, don't cover up the truth with boasting and lying. [15] *For jealousy and selfishness are not God's kind of wisdom. Such things are earthly, unspiritual, and demonic.* [16] *For wherever there is jealousy and selfish ambition, there you will find disorder and evil of every kind (James 3:14-16 NLT)."*

In such a situation, we can but pray for the Holy Spirit to free us from any venom in our hearts because when we acknowledge our shortcomings and ask for the Lord's help, He acts and flushes the bad out of our lives by putting us through a series of grueling and necessary tests that bring our own impurities to the surface. For some these processes can last weeks, months, years or decades until we are cleansed.

Now, if we return to 3:13, we can see that James is also telling his readers to have an understanding of God's ways. In the Old Testament, understanding is similar to wisdom in the sense that the word *sakal* in Hebrew means to act wisely or wisely understand. However, *sakal* carries other nuances, they include to be prudent, to be circumspect, or to navigate situations astutely.

Sakal also means to perceive, to look at, and pay attention to.

That all said, James wrote his letter in Greek and the word for understanding in James 3:13 is *epistēmōn,* which means to be endued with knowledge, to be expert in or learned. In other words, James is telling readers that we should aim to be thoroughly knowledgeable of our Lord God's ways.

To understand Christ's ways requires us to understand Him intimately. It is not enough to know who our Lord is or what He has done in the Bible, we have to know Him personally. Such knowledge grows when we serve Christ and have a relationship with our Lord God.

But we only learn to see Him for who He truly is in our lives if we dedicate time to contemplating on all of the things that Jesus has done for us since we were born. This takes our love to a deeper level. In fact, we discover new things that we never knew before about Christ when we think on Him. I think it would be impossible for me to count the number of times the Lord has steered me away from the rocks of life and guided me back to calm waters.

In short, intimacy in Christ is important to all of us if we are to know Him for who He really is. Moses knew the Lord and it was on a completely different level to that of the Israelites.

"He (The Lord) made known his ways to Moses, his deeds to the people of Israel (Psalm 103:7 NIV)."

This relationship is at its most intimate when we live and pray in the Spirit first thing in the morning. We all have the same access to the Lord, however, it really depends on what we are willing to do about serving or not. Are we prepared to wake up first thing in the morning to pray for hours, ministering, praising, worshipping, adoring, interceding and thanking the Lord, or do we just say a 15-second prayer and think we are covered for the day? Each response receives the merit it deserves, in other words, you reap what you sow.

Now, let's go back to James 3:13 because he is really challenging the Christian Jews of the first century to go beyond perceiving and knowing the Lord for who He is.

The standard is really high here because James is telling us to go further, keep pushing and prove that we are indeed wise and knowledgeable of our Lord's ways by "*living an honorable life, doing good works.*" There it is!

We must live a life that is worth living and we must be humble about it, and that this humility is more than human humility, this humility is derived from wisdom, in other words, this humility is based on God's level of humility and this humility is found in His wisdom.

Can we think of anyone who was more wise or humble than Christ? For the Lord not only wrote the book on love, wisdom, knowledge, humility, and patience, He is also the world's first and foremost authority on faithfulness, goodness, joy, kindness, self-control, gentleness, sacrifice, steadfastness, miracles, science, math, time, creation and everything else I haven't mentioned at this point, such as art, architecture, symmetry, poetry and so on. For He created and defined them all.

We can only strive to imitate what Christ achieved in such little time, for greatness starts with humility, and humility means less of us and more of Him.

Indeed, when we look at the Bible, we rapidly notice that humility is the first prerequisite towards developing a Christlike character. With humility comes wisdom (Proverbs 11:2). It is essential to sound Christian behavior as humility goes hand in hand with gentleness, patience and bearing with one another (Ephesians 4:2).

Humility is the first step to turning back to the Lord (2 Chronicles 7:14). On top of this, the Lord shows favor to the humble (James 4:6), gives guidance (Psalms 25:9) and crowns them with victory (Psalms 149:4). We must guard our hearts with humility and this is especially important for those who are in the service of the Lord.

There are no greater examples of humility and love than the Lord washing the feet of the disciples, humbling himself to the position of the lowliest servant in a household, only later to take this further and suffer humiliation on the Cross:

"Now that I, your Lord and Teacher, have washed your feet, you also should wash one another's feet. [15] I have set you an example that you should do as I have done for you. [16] Very truly I tell you, no servant is greater than his master, nor is a messenger greater than the one who sent him. [17] Now that you know these things, you will be blessed if you do them. (John 13:14-16 NIV).

Have you washed someone's feet? I must confess that I was not enthralled with such an idea at first and found it challenging until I did it, then and only then I found it liberating. It was as if I was being cleansed by the Lord as I washed the other person's foot. It is hard to describe but highly recommend it for humility is the starting point to walking with our Lord God after accepting Christ.

In short, Christ's going to the Cross is not a career opportunity but a divine calling to be part of our Lord God's mission on earth. To be used, taught, guided and commanded by the Creator of the universe is like nothing I have ever experienced in my life. No job can compare. It is beyond the sublime and awesome to watch. Paul shares a similar sentiment:

"For when I preach the gospel, I cannot boast, since I am compelled to preach. Woe to me if I do not preach the gospel! (1 Corinthians 9:16 NIV).

Oh the joy to play a role in the Lord's great plan for His people, however, here is a sad truth, so many are called to ministry but so few come. This is not good as Jesus commanded:

"Go and make disciples of all nations, baptizing them in the name of the Father and the Son and the Holy Spirit (Matthew 28:19 NIV)."

Did you notice the use of the imperative at the start of the verse? *"Go and make disciples,"* said the Lord. Jesus is telling us that we all need to tell others about Him. Now, can you imagine if everybody did this? The world would be a very different place. Sadly, though, and as before, many are called but few step up to the plate.

And this is the problem right here in James 3 because Christ's brother is not only saying that we should seek to be wise and know the Lord intimately, but we should also lead a good life by doing deeds in humility, while remembering Christ's command for us to go and make disciples of all nations.

That all said, we must also remember that ministry starts with our own children! They are so precious in the Lord's sight. I remember vividly when a six-year-old girl gave me a hug of joy because Jesus just healed her from life-threatening asthma. In the name of Jesus, she was cured. Her mother was also spared surgery after a hernia in her neck was cast out (Acts 19:12), yes cast out not cured.

Serving is incredibly exciting, it is an adventure, especially when you are guided by the Holy Spirit, you hear His commands and embrace His spiritual gifts to build up others. This is extremely powerful when you combine these gifts with the wisdom and knowledge of the Word of God. Ministry is so much more than going to the pulpit once a week. It is living a life that is worth living, serving richly in Christ day after day, and when that Sunday finally comes, you tell folk exactly what the Holy Spirit would have you proclaim about Jesus Christ and His Word of God!

For we are here to announce the Good News to the afflicted, pray for the brokenhearted, declare liberty to the captives, remind them of the day of vengeance of the Lord, comfort all who mourn, encourage the downtrodden, cause former captives to become trees of righteousness, and support others through intercession to help them rebuild shattered lives, bringing restoration and prosperity.

And we do all this for the glory of the Lord, for Ministry is a life that one leads because of our love for Christ. It is not a role that one plays out to the delight of others. Ministry transfers life, brings emotional and physical healing to others and offers rewards that we could never imagine but can it be tough? Does the Lord test us? Yes, for sure.

For Christ is transforming us into Him as He brings our impurities up to the surface, exposes our hidden warts and heals our broken hearts!

For when we know who we are in Christ, when we learn that we were never created to be subjugated or oppressed by the world or others, we discover freedom in Him, we come across a new and true purpose for our lives and inevitably pray to ask the Lord how we can serve.

So instead of living our busy lives to the point of digital overload and distraction, we should put our smartphones down and focus on living our lives together to the fullest, fixing our eyes and thoughts on Christ, placing all of our confidence in His immense grace, unwavering care and immeasurable love because He really loves us and how. He is always with us and that never changes.

Peter sums this up best: "[7] *The end of all things is near. Therefore be alert and of sober mind so that you may pray.* [8] *Above all, love each other deeply, because love covers over a multitude of sins.* [9] *Offer hospitality to one another without grumbling.* [10] *Each of you should use whatever gift you have received to serve others, as faithful stewards of God's grace in its various forms.* [11] *If anyone speaks, they should do so as one who speaks the very words of God. If anyone serves, they should do so with the strength God provides, so that in all things God may be praised through Jesus Christ. To him be the glory and the power for ever and ever. Amen (1 Peter 4:7-11 NIV)."*

Love and live richly in Christ before the Rapture, for Revival is coming before we are all taken up! However, not all Christians are going. In fact, millions upon millions will be left behind and that takes us to our penultimate warning from the Lord.

Chapter 9
Jesus is coming but God the Father will also be upset

"[37] For yet a little while, and he that shall come will come, and will not tarry. [38] Now the just shall live by faith: but if any man draw back, my soul shall have no pleasure in him (Hebrews 10:37-38 KJV)."

Before that service on the Rapture in August 2023, the Lord gave me one final message - Hebrews 10:37-38. It was the Lord's final warning to our church in Brazil and serves as a red light to millions and millions of Christians, who live out of relationship with the Lord. The warning was simply this, Jesus is coming back and we cannot risk being unprepared for He is coming no matter what! However, if we are caught out because we are unprepared for His return, our Heavenly Father is not going to be happy about it!

Let's break down these verses further and focus on what matters most. Firstly, Jesus is coming back and nothing is going to change that because this is the Heavenly Father's sovereign will and what He determines, goes. However, I have a question. Is Jesus' pending return news to you?

It is interesting the reactions I get when I ask this question. For the few where I live in Brazil here, they have no view on the matter. They have no expectation. Jesus might as well be returning in 500 years from now for all they know or care. However, there are those, and they are many, who nod their heads in agreement, admit the Lord is coming and acknowledge it is just a question of time.

They are then quick to note that the world is also coming at an end and that they feel this because they hear it in their hearts. Where are you on this point? Do you hear the inaudible whispers of the Holy Spirit talking to your spirit? Or do you hardly ever pray and do not know?

Either way, Jesus is coming back. Glory be to the Lord. Ring the church bells for the wait is almost over. Glorious will be that day, the day of Jesus Christ!

There will be rapturous joy across Heaven that day to see the Lord put rout to the enemy once and for all. Vengeance is the Lord's indeed. The world will mourn but His people will be jubilant! Glorious will also be the day of the Rapture that comes before His return. It will be glorious for the Father, the Son and the Holy Spirit.

However, our Lord God is going to be really upset with those who are left behind. He will be deeply aggrieved with the lost - the unbelievers who denied Christ and the baptized who failed to make Jesus a priority in their lives. They are not the few, however. There are millions and millions of struggling unprotected out-of-relationship unchurched Christians, who are just growing in number at this time.

They are completely unaware that they are in a spiritual battle that they are at risk of completely losing. Baptism alone is not enough to save them at the time of Rapture. Now, I am not going to use this opportunity to warn of the horrors of hell. We have covered this already. No, I would like to impress on you to impress on others that the Kingdom of God is absolutely amazing and gorgeous – it is beyond our dreams, and the unchurched are our lost brothers and sisters who need to be brought back to the fold because they are royalty, they have an eternal crown, throne, and mansion waiting for them.

Their names are carved on a stone that symbolizes that they have been acquitted of their past sins on earth. They are going to miss out in a huge way for they will never know what it means to live in blissful peace and joy, walking down streets of gold and basking in the love of the Father and the Son. The Kingdom of God is incomparable, it is the home of our Lord God and He has held nothing back, it is beautiful, it is awesome, it is divine and the unchurched are putting all of this eternal future at risk.

Who in their right mind would give up such an opportunity? And yet so many do not even know it exists. This is the sad truth but how bleak is this situation?

The reasons why someone loses spiritual connection are many. Some leave the church because they were never connected to the Lord in the first place.

Why? They never knew who Jesus really is, they never personally experienced His love, His forgiveness, His strength and power, they never felt Him because they never adopted any real spiritual habits that brought them closer to Him and vice-versa.

There was no daily anointing in their lives, they withered spiritually and died out! Or perhaps the reason was more simple, they were hurt, offended or sidelined by others in the church or by a pastor, and this bitterness grew into unforgiveness, prompting departure from that congregation.

Maybe, they wanted a quick solution to finding God in their lives and it had become an insurmountable task in their minds – so they gave up and went abroad looking for God in a statue. It could also be because a church was tolerating sinful behavior in a few and this led to bitterness and condemnation from others because the matter was not addressed.

Or worse yet, apathy and unbelief crept in! Or perhaps, the thinking is that going to church at Christmas and Easter is already enough for mum and dad and the kids – and who has time for anything anyway? Who cares, really, because Jesus is going to forgive us all anyway, right? Doesn't He forgive sinners? Isn't that what Christ does?

Not with the Rapture. Insincere hearts do not get to go. They will face the Great Tribulation and suffer the fury of the Lord for all eternity. What we do here and now echoes into never-ending time, for the unchurched cannot be saved by their own self-righteousness, good deeds, or hope in their own works. Faith in self is eternal suicide.

Money is not going to work either. For everything is from the Lord and of the Lord, this includes our money, homes and loved ones. Christ needs none of these things because they are already His. And lastly, we servants of the Lord cannot transfer our faith onto others or share part of our salvation so that they will be saved too.

We can but pray and intercede with the Lord, however, if the unchurched stay away, what happens next? Where does that leave them on the day of the Rapture?

Simply put, they are at high risk of being left behind, and arguably, the saddest aspect of this upcoming Rapture will be keenly felt by those Christians who walked away from Christ but did not even know it. They had no idea.

They thought that attending a few services a year, a prayer here and there, was enough to be saved. They never picked up their Cross and thought that they had done enough! Oh how sad that day of Rapture will be for them! My heart goes out to them. So how high is the risk for the unchurched?

Are we talking about hundreds of millions of Christians or hundreds of millions out of nearly 2.4 billion Christians in the world today? I do not know, for we cannot know what is in the hearts of believers.

I have a question, however, if you were the one to go to the Cross in the place of Jesus, how would you feel afterward if the people you were supposed to save just ignored you? I can imagine that we, like the Lord, would *"have no pleasure"* in such folk either, especially on the day of the Rapture. Let's review that key verse again:

"37 For yet a little while, and he that shall come will come, and will not tarry. 38 Now the just shall live by faith: but if any man draw back, my soul shall have no pleasure in him (Hebrews 10:37-38 NIV)."

The Lord will have no pleasure because that person drew back. In other words, the Lord was rejected. For that soul at least, Christ's incredible act of love on the Cross was dismissed for naught. But what are the consequences of such an action?

To be baptized and then reject the Lord is tantamount to insulting the Holy Spirit and utterly disparages what Jesus did on the Cross. Worse yet, so many do it through unrepentant, conscious and hardened opposition to the truth of Christ. We are after all living the Great Apostasy! You see, this scenario is exactly the opposite to what the Heavenly Father wants for and from His people.

To understand the sheer peril of taking such a course of action, we need only go back eight verses in the same chapter to see how our Lord reacts to such a situation:

"[29] *How much more severely do you think someone deserves to be punished who has trampled the Son of God underfoot, who has treated as an* **unholy** *thing the blood of the covenant that sanctified them, and who has insulted the Spirit of grace?* [30] *For we know him who said, 'It is mine to avenge; I will repay,' and again, 'The Lord will judge his people' (Hebrews 10:29-30 NIV).*"

A massive red flag is raised here. I fear the Lord and find these verses to be some of the scariest in the whole Bible. When you read them in context with what happened to Miriam, Korah, Dathan and Abiram and the Israelites respectively in Numbers 12, 16, and 14, you will understand where I am coming from. Miriam temporarily became a leper, Korah, Dathan and Abiram were swallowed up after the earth opened up beneath them, and the grumbling Israelites, who had seen the miracles that the Lord had performed in Egypt, were sentenced to hardship in the desert until their very deaths. They never saw the promised land.

All of these chapters speak to man's defiance against the Lord's authority. Miriam attacked Moses' authority and consequently - albeit unknowingly - attacked the Lord's authority. Korah, Dathan and Abiram also attacked Moses' authority and consequently attacked the Lord's authority. And the Israelites?

Same problem as they started to talk of choosing another leader to go back to Egypt. When we attack those in delegated authority (i.e. those who have been given authority to lead in a church, school, marriage, hospital and so on), we are attacking the Lord's authority.

In short, we rebel. And when we walk away and reject Christ, we quickly find ourselves in defiant opposition to the Lord. The result? We inevitably end up attacking God's authority whether we realize this or not.

This is the worst place that an unchurched Christian can be in. To attack the Lord's authority is Satanic. How come? Lucifer, once ordained as a guardian cherub, became filled with pride and exalted himself above the Lord – and in doing so, attacked the Lord's authority (Isaiah 14:13-14). Lucifer, who was filled with wickedness, was expelled from heaven and cast down to earth.

It is important for Christians to know that it is by the Lord's authority that we are still here and exist at all, and the greatest mistake we can make is to attack the Lord's authority – for we do so at great peril but you dear reader may think that the Lord no longer does this sort of thing anymore and that this is scaremongering.

Really? Opening the ground to swallow up people? Leprosy? Nah, that was in the Old Testament, these things no longer happen. Here' is the rub - absolutely nothing happens without the Lord's permission. Remember Satan had to ask permission from the Lord to test Job (Job1:12, 2:6)? Everything is by the Lord's authority and permission.

When we understand this, we look at the world differently. Earthquakes, floods, global warming and plagues are all by His permission. Indeed, if we dig deeper, we finally come to see that our lives are in the balance and that our support, or rather our very foothold in life, comes from the Lord. It is by His authority and permission that we are still here.

Cue Deuteronomy 32:35: "*Their foot shall slide in due time.*" This verse says it all. The foot – which represents our grip on our very own life – is supported by the Lord. By the will of the Father, the Lord can remove that support at any moment that He chooses.

We clearly see here that there is a very thin line between life and death when we make ourselves the god of our own lives. Such an attitude or way of life puts an unchurched soul in a precarious position. Will it be eternal condemnation or salvation for that person?

The Lord will respect that person's free will. This is very precious and important to Him. Christ will not interfere, but He will do everything to bring a person back into a relationship with Him. With time the Lord will act and if He does, there are a number of tactics He will use. Usually, it starts with friends and family inviting an unchurched person back to church. Sometimes, the Lord could send a future spouse, who is a fervent Christian.

Or the Lord will send pastors to the unchurched person. They could bump into each other in the street, for example. Prayers are said, sins are confessed, blessings are made. This is what I term as the Good Cop scenario. However, what if the unchurched person continues to persist and does not return to church?

Well, then we will see what I call the Bad Cop strategy. The Lord allows financial crisis to set in, a job is lost, or about to be lost, or a person goes to hospital – his or her life is in the balance. In short, the measures become more and more drastic. So, allow me to tell you a tale of what the Lord does when He decides the time has come to bring an unchurched soul back to Him.

I remember sitting opposite a woman, who was traumatized after being kidnapped for an hour at gunpoint. She was mugged in her car as the robbers emptied all of her money and maxed out her credit card. That person, who remains nameless, had clearly become a shadow of her former self by the time she came to us at church. Disheveled, distraught, her face was blotchy from crying earlier.

As I sat there at the back of the church with her, I asked myself why the Holy Spirit had put me in front of her. I had had no experience with muggings. I had never dealt with trauma victims, and I knew nothing about this woman. I had never met her before in my life either. These thoughts raced through my mind as she told of her one-hour plight in the car.

There was despair in her eyes and voice. I looked on sympathetically and asked the Lord to help me understand better. *Then the Holy Spirit told me why.*

I looked at the woman and smiled. She kept talking but I gently interrupted her and said, "I think what I am about to tell you is going to help you." She stopped talking and looked at me. "The Lord allowed the kidnapping to happen." She looked at me in shock. I continued:

"You were baptized, you used to go to church but you had stopped going and the Lord knew you were never going to go back to church. This is why the Lord allowed you to be kidnapped, to shock you so that you would come back and it worked because you are now here at church. He did this out of love." She looked at me, she didn't understand.

"If the Lord hadn't removed His protection and allowed you to be kidnapped, you would have finished your life in hell instead of living with Jesus for all eternity, your kidnapping was a blessing, it was a deliverance from spending eternity in hell, you are back in church and you are saved because you had forsaken the Lord," I added.

Her eyes widened.

"You would never have come back to church if it had not been for the kidnapping, would you?" I asked. She nodded, she had no plan to ever return to church. "In fact, you were never in trouble, the Lord allowed the kidnapping to happen, but they were never going to shoot you. The whole plan was to shock you into coming back to church and nothing more." At that moment, I literally saw the weight coming off of her shoulders. Her invisible struggle of the heart and mind was over.

The following week, she was back in church and was another person. Completely changed. She was smiling, had dressed well and had clearly been to the hairdresser. Two weeks later, I prayed with her again. She never once mentioned her ordeal at gunpoint. It was as if it had never happened. Instead, she was at that point more worried about her marriage than anything else!

In the end, she had learned that it is our Lord God who guides our steps, and should He decide to remove His protection, then we must know that this is done in love – no matter how great the punishment may seem at the time. However, if the Lord has tried all of the stops and the unchurched soul has not responded in kind, then we often see a person being blessed in the final months or weeks of his or her life before it is ended. Just like that, gone. No more.

This is why there is no such thing as the gospel of tomorrow, because, for some of us, there may be no tomorrow. The pandemic showed us just how fragile life is.

So what about the Rapture? What will happen? Will millions be left behind? Tens of millions? Hundreds of millions? You can bet that Christ is going to do His utmost to save us from our own rebellious ways. For Christ did not go to the Cross in vain! Christ obviously prefers that we take the high road and live in a relationship in Him, to be obedient in love, sacrifice, trust, faith, dependence and service.

We are His people and if we let Him, He will prepare us for the next life through the excellent guidance of the Holy Spirit. The closer we are to the Lord, the better it is for us. Spiritual connection ensues and increasing spiritual depth is the consequence – provided we make the effort and keep it up.

Whatever that final number is – you dear reader must make sure that you and those who you love and care about are not among those who stay behind.

This is why it is critically important to be in a relationship with Christ because there will not be enough time on that final day. We must all live honorably and peacefully in a relationship with Christ. We must do His works out of love, sharing with others what we have, helping the oppressed and others in all humility, and learning under the Holy Spirit's guidance and tutelage to be considerate, merciful, sincere, content and joyful no matter what the circumstances.

We must carry our own Cross and die to the self instead of gambling with our salvation, which is not just based on accepting Christ, having faith in Him, but also living a life in Him and for Him. Other pastors and Christians may disagree. Jesus said Himself that we need only believe to be saved. Yes, that is the first condition and promise as spelled out here in a favorite verse of mine:

"To open their eyes, so they may turn from darkness to light and from the power of Satan to God. Then they will receive forgiveness for their sins and be given a place among God's people, who are set apart by faith in me (Acts 26:18 NIV)."

Just believe and you are saved. However, there are three key words in this verse, *"so they may turn."* To turn is a process in itself until it is completed. We do not just turn from darkness to light within a split second (unless you are Paul of course – he did it in less than 20 seconds Acts 9:4-9). It is a process. For some it can take decades.

What matters is that we make the effort to turn but we cannot do that alone, we need the Holy Spirit and that requires relationship, getting down on our knees in humility and saying, "Lord, turn me into the person that you would have me be."

For the Lord called on all of us to pick up our own Crosses and follow Him. The Cross does not come without sacrifice and to follow Him is a rallying call for all of us to enter into a relationship with Christ. However, should this still irk you dear reader or others, then take your concerns and pleas to the Lord, in fact I encourage you to wrestle with Him rather than with a fellow brother in Christ.

However, before you do, contemplate the truth of the following verses about the importance of being in a relationship with Christ: John 15:4-5, John 17:3, Colossians 3:1-3, Hebrews 2:1, Hebrews 2:3, Revelation 2:3, Revelation 3:15-16, Revelation 3:18-20, Matthew 6:24, Matthew 4:4, Matthew 6:33, Matthew 22:37 Luke 14:16-27, John 6:44, John 6:48, John 14:15, John 16:33, Galatians 2:20, Romans 7:4, 1 Corinthians 1:9 (I love this one), Hebrews 3:12-14, and this one I love, Titus 2:11-14 NIV:

"11 For the grace of God has appeared that offers salvation to all people. 12 It teaches us to say "No" to ungodliness and worldly passions, and to live self-controlled, upright and godly lives in this present age, 13 while we wait for the blessed hope—the appearing of the glory of our great God and Savior, Jesus Christ, 14 who gave himself for us to redeem us from all wickedness and to purify for himself a people that are his very own, eager to do what is good."

This text speaks much about the need for relationship with Christ, personal transformation and purification because this is what Christ is doing – He is preparing His people for that final day when every knee shall bow to the Lord and be His (Romans 14:11). Until then, Christ is purifying *"for himself a people that are his very own, eager to do what is good."*

It takes time to purify someone, and this will only move as fast as that person wants it to move. This process of a person being purified, or rather becoming more holy, is better known as sanctification, and it is only possible when that person is in a relationship with Christ and is calling on the Lord to become a better Christians.

For only a relationship built on faith in Christ will save us on the day of the Rapture. So, let's never forget, the Lord will only alert those who are in a relationship with Him that the Rapture is about to happen. Remember we looked at the implications of such a scenario earlier in the book and what happens if you are next to a loved one who has not received the Rapture warning from the Holy Spirit.

Get that person to confess his or her sins and forgive whoever needs to be forgiven, and fast! Really! It matters. Every last second matters! Every soul matters. This is very real. If this book saves one soul because of this tip in this paragraph, it will have been worth the effort of writing it! For this is the message that the Lord has put into my heart, relationship, relationship, relationship in Christ saves.

And this is why we should pray for the unchurched, for their salvation but we should also pray for church leaders, who are either under continuous attack from all sides or have caved under pressure or the need to be popular and consequently lost sight of our Lord God's values. The pressure on all of us to get it right is immense. The pressure to pay the bills. The pressure to do the Lord's will.

For the mission of salvation is Christ's, the glory of this mission is the Father's and He shares His glory with no one. If we are trying by our own human efforts, we must breathe, stop and consult the Lord lest we sweat – for this is not the will of God!

'[18] They are to wear linen turbans on their heads and linen undergarments around their waists. They must not wear anything that makes them perspire (Ezekiel 44:18 NIV)."

Churches are not lit by profane fire but with the Fire of God (Leviticus 9:23-10:2). Pastors, priests and vicars, who do not preach the Word according to our Lord God, will find that the blood of others will be on their hands (Ezekiel 3:18). This is why Paul said in Acts 20:26, that *"he is innocent of the blood of any of you."*

Paul made sure that every soul he met understood the Good News – the gospel of Christ, the gospel of the Kingdom of God. Consequently, he visited many cities but spent in some of these places a year or more at a time to not only plant churches but to ensure that brothers and sisters understood the message of Christ.

Today, all brothers and sisters in Christ have a role in bringing back the unchurched to the Lord while reaching out to the unsaved in His name. For, we must all personally know Jesus in our lives and grow in the Lord *"until we all come to such unity in our faith and knowledge of God's Son that we will be mature in the Lord, measuring up to the full and complete standard of Christ (Ephesians 4:13 NIV)."*

But what about those who are in a relationship with our Lord Christ. How should we proceed? We covered much about this in the last chapter, but to recap, we should prepare for the end and treat every day as if it were the last, living it richly and vividly in love and service. We cannot not waste our time, for *"time is short, and the time is now"* the Lord told me in March 2024 and has since repeated the same message on numerous occasions. Time is so precious because it is finite. Eternity with the Lord is never-ending time but our time, here and now, is finite and it defines our eternity. For the Lord's clock is ticking down to that final moment when the last soul on earth confesses and accepts Christ as Lord and savior, triggering the Rapture. So where does that leave us?

For those in relationship, we must hold onto our identities in Christ. When the Lord looks at us, we are not identified by our political choices, we are not identified by our sexuality, we are not identified by the stars or the astrological signs, we are not identified or defined by the football team we support, we are not defined by our jobs or the achievements or failures at work, we are not defined by friends, colleagues or family, or by how much money we have in our bank accounts, the size of our homes or the speed of our cars, or whether we eat too many doughnuts and chocolate, or anything else on this planet. We are identified and defined by our Lord God and there is no identification or definition more perfect than what our Lord has willed for us for before the Holy Spirt formed us in our mother's womb, our Lord "*knew you. Before you were born, I set you apart (Jeremiah 1:5 NIV)."*

For we are not CEOs, janitors or waiters. In Christ, we are created in God's image and likeness, we must have dominion over all earth for we are kings of the earth, and as children of Christ, the King of kings, we are the pinnacle of creation (this can and should never be demeaned). For we must remember that when arguing with someone, especially someone we love, we are really arguing someone who was created by the Lord in His image. That should stop us long enough to take a deep breath and reassess the situation for the Lord loves you and the person you are arguing with, and there is nothing worse for God the Father to see His children in

Christ squabble, for when we come to Christ, we are part of His royal family.

We are to govern and cultivate the land and protect it from evil in obedience to the Lord. We have a nature of our own, the Lord absolutely respects this (this is why people send themselves to hell because they reject Christ), but we are called to love one another *"fervently with pure hearts (1 Peter 1:22 NIV)"* and serve Him first as well as each other, praising (His great deeds) and worshipping the Lord for who He is (and not only for what He has done).

The Lord has a plan for us all, for we are justified (accepted and chosen) by Him, for He loved us first to be priests in His Kingdom and Holy nation, for we are a part of His people, His most treasured possession. We are called to be holy in our conduct, to rejoice always, pray constantly, give thanks, not quench the Spirit, not despise prophetic messages but test them. We are all called to complete the race, by keeping away from every type of evil and persevering in Christ. Peter has much to say on this!

"[5] For this very reason, make every effort to add to your faith goodness; and to goodness, knowledge; [6] and to knowledge, self-control; and to self-control, perseverance; and to perseverance, godliness; [7] and to godliness, mutual affection; and to mutual affection, love (2 Peter 1:5-7 NIV)."

And when we depart, we will receive a crown and an "*incorruptible and undefiled*" inheritance that "*does not fade*" and is "*reserved*" for all of us in the next life (1 Peter 1:4-16). To understand more about the rewards in our next life, check out Revelation chapters 2 and 3 and the promises that Jesus makes, including *"the right to sit with me (Christ) on my throne, just as I was victorious and sat down with my Father on his throne (Revelation 3:21 NIV)."*

We all need to keep our eyes and thoughts focused on Christ, His values and not society's values, and let our Lord God transform us into the best version of ourselves as the antichrist prepares the world for his short reign. For in the same way that the Lord has a mission for us all, the devil has unsurprisingly an anti-mission for us all too. In this spiritual war, the enemy's anti-mission is to move us as far away as possible from Jesus in any way possible.

It can be as subtle as watching Netflix at night or as obvious as someone vehemently denying Christ while foaming at the mouth. Atheism and existentialism are some of the religions of reason that the enemy uses, while he employs his billions (yes billions) of spirits to speak to our souls, confuse our minds and blind us to the truths about our Lord and what He did on the Cross. Spiritualism is one of those many religions. It is seductive.

People through mediums can access so-called "good spirits," however, in so doing, those same spirits or their buddies take residence in the lives of such admirers, blinding them from the truth of the Lord and in worst-case scenarios leading their victims to suicide.

Arguably, the most powerful strategy used by the enemy today in this digital age is distraction. The smartphone is the culprit as it provides immediate distraction. Who can be bothered to wait 30 seconds or more to hear the Lord in prayer when you can have video games, films and food on tap. We do not even have to go out anymore.

Isolation is perfect for the enemy – especially when Christians are called to commune with the Lord and each other! Another is to encourage folk to believe in God the Father but deny God the Son. This is because if you accept the Father but deny the Son, then you also deny the Father (1 John 2:23), and for the Father that "believer" is not righteous, is not saved and not protected for he or she has rejected the Son.

No one can get into heaven unless they are covered with the blood of Christ, for God the Son covers us in righteousness and when we are in Him, the Heavenly Father sees Christ in us (1 Corinthians 1:30 NLT), and not our litany of sins that we can never pay ourselves for "*no one can redeem the life of another or give to God a ransom for them – the ransom for a life is costly, no payment is ever enough (Psalm 49:7-8 (NIV).*"

So, know this, the enemy is going to do everything to distract us from Christ so that we fall out of relationship with Him and are left behind after the Rapture! That is all it takes for Satan to win. We must be wise to avoid the many pitfalls and snares that the enemy has set for us. But are we really in a spiritual war? Absolutely. Put on the armor of God daily brothers and sisters! It is so important, especially when you lay your hands on others to pray! We all need spiritual protection and authority in the name of Jesus.

When I suit up for battle on a daily basis, I say out loud that I am putting on the armor of God, this way the enemy knows that I am ready for battle. It is an unseen battle but an important one.

How often I have wondered how Jesus could just cast out every single demon on the planet and end this spiritual war with one command or breath, however, He does not, nor does the Holy Spirit, because the Lord respects our free will so much!

Lots of people love evil. Lots of people love sin. Lots of people want to be depressed. Lots of people do not want to be cured, really! We must respect this, as hard as it is, and instead draw on the weapons of spiritual warfare to fight the good fight to take down the demonic strongholds that hold our brothers and sisters captive:

"[12] For the word of God is alive and active. Sharper than any double-edged sword, it penetrates even to dividing soul and spirit, joints and marrow; it judges the thoughts and attitudes of the heart. [13] Nothing in all creation is hidden from God's sight. Everything is uncovered and laid bare before the eyes of him to whom we must give account (Hebrews 4:12-13 NIV)."

As believers, we too must stay close to the Word of God to avoid the many traps and keep inching closer to Jesus, and while we feel more sinful during such a process, the Lord will come closer to us. For He means to change us all and make us more like Him, to mature us, grow us, evolve us.

It is beautiful to watch others be changed by the Lord – we become complete opposites. Ebeneezer Scrooge was no caricature. The Lord transforms Scrooge's into real Christians every day worldwide. So how do we move closer and protect ourselves from the enemy?

Praying and reading the Bible are the two most important things we can do as Christians in our own time.

We must pray in the Holy Spirit on all occasions with all kinds of prayers and requests, we must be alert and also keep on praying for all of the Lord's people (Ephesians 6:18 paraphrased).

However, how can we do that if we are too busy just being busy with things we do not even remember we did the day before? Where is the value in that type of lifestyle? How do we learn to listen to the Lord, to connect, grow and discover who Christ is in our lives if we are incapable of praying for more than 15 to 30 seconds at a time? And what is prayer in the Holy Spirit anyway, what did Paul mean by that in his letter to the Ephesians? Many say it is to speak in tongues and pray in our minds simultaneously. If you can do this, the benefits of this are huge because we are called to hear the Lord as we pray, for prayer is a dialogue, and praying in tongues facilitates our ability in hearing what the Holy Spirit has to say. But wait, there is a truth here.

Paul the Apostle made it clear that not everybody will have every gift from the Holy Spirit. Some will be able to talk in tongues and others will not have that ability. So what happens then? Did Paul really mean that praying in the Spirit is praying in tongues? When we consider that so many Christians do not speak in tongues, it would not make much sense to conclude that praying in the Spirit means praying in tongues.

Prayer is for everybody. Having looked up numerous references on what it means to pray in the Spirit, I realized that it would be difficult to accept such opposing opinions that either argue in favor of talking in tongues or against it. How could I know the reliability of a source? If someone speaks in tongues, it is likely they are going to recommend that approach, and those who do not will not recommend speaking in tongues. Instead, I asked the Lord.

The message came and Christ explained that to pray in the Spirit is to *"pray in me."* There was a pause as I prayed softly in tongues. The message continued, to pray in the Spirit is *"to pray in trust. To pray according to my will. To pray for all things at all times. To believe in the words that you pray. To exercise faith that I will act. To know that I hear every word but I may or may not act on it."*

He then concluded, we must *"turn over all things to the Lord."* There are a number of key points here, one of them being that we must pray in trust and believe that the impossible will happen, however, we must also know that the Lord may or may not act on what we pray.

We know that the Lord will act if it is in the interest and benefit to the Kingdom of God. However, the key to knowing whether He will act or not is in what He said earlier, that we must pray according to His will.

The only way to pray according to His will is to ask Him, and I have found that hearing the voice of the Lord is not something that comes naturally, it takes time, patience, training and I have to admit, it is a lot easier to do it when talking in tongues! We must all persevere, not lose heart or give up, however, this is why it is so important to have Christian friends around you – to pray for you and to be used by the Lord to deliver His messages to you if you do not yet hear His voice directly in your life!

To hear the Lord's voice takes time and training. Meditation helps us with this endeavor. It took me more than two years of meditation. After I started speaking in tongues, my ability to understand the Lord's voice just clicked into place. For when we can hear the Lord's will in our lives and for the lives of others, our priorities shift for the better toward Him as our minds are continuously renewed, our Spirits are attuned to hearing the Holy Spirit and we learn of God's good, pleasing and perfect will for our lives!

There is more, though, we must also dedicate time to studying the Bible for the knowledge of the truth will set us all free (John 8:32). When we do not know the truth, we are at high risk of not growing and are susceptible to false teachers. In other words, without the knowledge of the truth, we will not be free and we will sway like reeds in the water, moved more by our perceptions of the world than what our Lord God intends for us.

So be very wary these coming years for we must stay in Christ and remain under His protection. Going to church increases our protection, especially if you have a pastor, who can pray and fast with you!

So, dear reader, what do you feel about the end? Have you yet challenged yourself with this question? Do you even welcome it? Are you prepared? Are those around you unchurched or unsaved? Have you made a decision about Christ yet? Keep reading, as we will see Christ's message in the next chapter about that final day of Rapture!

Let's recap! Those who are in relationship with our Lord Jesus Christ of Nazareth will receive an alert from the Holy Spirit, God the Spirit, that the Rapture is about to happen and they *will* be raptured. We will have a minute or so to repent, confess our sins, renew our faith in Christ and then let others know before we are gone.

Say this prayer on this glorious day: "I (your name) confess the sins I remember, do not remember and do not know (confess your sins in your head or out loud – the Lord hears either way), and I ask for forgiveness from the Lord Jesus Christ, and I forgive those that have hurt me and turn over any grudges to the Lord, for I am ready Lord, for your glory Jesus Christ, for I am yours and you are mine!"

At this point, call out to others (if they are not already praying with you the same prayer of confession and forgiveness), and look out of the window or go outside, and wait to see the Fire of God's lights of amber and bright yellowish-white streaks flickering like the blue and white colors that reflect from a swimming pool onto a wall.

Wait for the first one, and look around for the last time, say if you want, "for your glory Jesus, glory hallelujah to the Lord," then wait for a beam of amber to surround you before you feel a jerk – just like a train starting to move but the jerk is vertical (upward) – and you are instantaneously taken up to New Jerusalem. Praise be to God! However, is that it? Are we finished?

No, not at all. In the final week of writing this book, our Lord God Jesus Christ gave me one last warning, and this for me is the big one and completes the vision. Take heed and woe to those who are left behind!

Chapter 10
Jesus Christ's Final Warning
- What will happen to you if you are left behind after the Rapture –

"Behold, I am coming like a thief! Blessed is the one who stays awake, keeping his garments on, that he may not go about naked and be seen exposed! (Revelation 16:15 NIV)."

So are you excited, intrigued and curious or just dreading the Rapture and subsequent return of the Lord! Do you have a firm view on this? Has the Lord spoken to your heart about the end yet? Do you feel it could be this year of 2024 or just a decade away, if anything at all? If you are not quite there yet, I leave you with a final message from our Lord Jesus Christ of Nazareth.

You see, while writing this book between September 2023 and April 2024, the Lord started to answer a series of questions about this book the Rapture. I was still asking myself whether I should go forward with the book in January of 2024. Should I give up? I had asked that question several times. At that point I was intensely rewriting chapter five. This is what Jesus Christ told me:

"Keep writing, do not stop. The people must know the message that I have to give to them. Do not stop… Time is short, the time is now. Do not waste it. The book must continue and be finished as soon as possible. I will help you finish it. Keep praying in the Spirit for there is more to come."

Now, this message hit me on several levels. I had slowed down the process of writing the book and the Lord was telling me not to waste time, but more importantly, the words, "*I will help you finish it*" just stuck in my mind.

As I continued to write the book, those words did not go away and eventually they morphed into another message, "*I will write the ending for you.*"

By Tuesday April 9, I felt that I had reached the end of the book and while I could have written more about relationship in Christ, ministry and what it means to be a Christian at the end of the church's existence on earth, I prayed that night in the Holy Spirit and the Lord Jesus Christ of Nazareth answered with his final message on the Rapture, and I share it here – exactly as it came to me, word for word, for this is the will of the Heavenly Father, for we must all be saved!

This is the final warning from our Lord Jesus Christ:

"The time is coming when I will return. Before that, my people will be raptured, they will be taken up. Everybody must be prepared. Everybody must know what is going to come. It will not be easy on those who will be left behind. They will suffer much. Regret, pain, hurt, anger and so much more will mark their lives like fresh wounds to the heart. Trust in me for I am coming and nothing can stop that, nothing can change that. Salvation cannot be bought, salvation is a gift in Me. It is time for people to take this very seriously because the consequences are terrible. I cannot underscore this enough. There will be great pain on this day. So much confusion. So much panic, uncertainty. There will be those who will kill themselves, for some it will be too great to bear. Families will be torn apart. There will be accidents and fires everywhere, the world will not be able to cope, it will collapse. The world will mourn this day. For everybody will know somebody who left. I cannot stress the importance of being in a relationship in Me. You will not want to be left behind."

It is chilling what the Lord said. Take a moment to reread this message again and again, to understand just how devastating the Rapture will be on those who are left behind, for those who will have to deal with families that will be torn apart - for everybody will know somebody who left.

Indeed, there will be those who will be unable to bear the situation and will end their lives, and what about those who will have to deal with a world that has just collapsed within the space of 100 to 150 milliseconds! We did not do very well as a race in 2001 after the Twin Towers collapsed. We suffered much in the 2008-2009 recession and what about the pandemic? That took its toll and still affects folk to this day.

Now, having read the Lord's message, just imagine the Rapture, for the greatest airlift in the history of this world will be devastating, utterly devastating.

If you are still coming to terms with what the Rapture means for you dear reader and your family, then I urge you – no matter what – to finish your journey in a relationship with Christ - for your eternity depends on it! If you are an unbeliever and reading this, know in your heart that salvation is a free gift that you will receive when you confess Jesus Christ as your Lord and Savior! Confess Him today, not tomorrow, get baptized and then pursue a relationship in Christ! For this is what the Lord wants above all because He does not want to see anyone left behind.

Until then, the Lord has made it clear that "*everybody must be prepared. Everybody must know*" about the Rapture. This is a command to all. If you are a pastor, minister, priest or missionary and the Lord spoke to your heart as your read this book, or you have prayed on this matter and heard from the Lord further, then I urge you to let "*everybody know.*"

If you are a Christian brother or sister, wondering what to do about all of this, just tell others that Christ is coming back and to prepare for the Rapture. While it will be terrible for those who are left behind, it will be glorious for those who are taken up to New Jerusalem. Do not be part of the Noah generation that stays on the ground!

For me, I am no longer worried about my mortgage and no longer put money into my pension. I am not advocating you to do the same. Believe what you believe, but just stay in a relationship with Christ, be prepared daily by renewing your faith in Christ, confessing to the Lord and living richly in Him daily.

Until the Rapture, ask the Lord to use you to minister to the Lord (praise Him for His deeds, worship Him for who He is and pray to Him) and intercede for others (pray for them and their needs), and remember to "*not store up for yourselves treasures on earth, where moths and vermin destroy, and where thieves break in and steal.* [20] *But store up for yourselves treasures in heaven, where moths and vermin do not destroy, and where thieves do not break in and steal.* [21] *For where your treasure is, there your heart will be also (Matthew 6:19-21 NIV).*"

Lastly, I trust that the revelations in this book will help you and your family prepare for the end and strengthen your relationship in Christ or (re)start one. I also hope that you will be inspired to tell others about the coming return of Christ and the need to prepare for the Rapture.

For He is coming and nothing will change that. In the interim, God bless and if we never meet, the Lord be with your spirit, and grace of the Lord Jesus be with you all brothers and sisters, for Christ loved us first. Instead, I hope to see you in eternity, for the time has come, the Kingdom of God is very near, repent and believe!

Now, I must bow out and leave you with Peter's last words that so aptly summarize this book and what we must do:

"8 But do not forget this one thing, dear friends: With the Lord a day is like a thousand years, and a thousand years are like a day. 9 The Lord is not slow in keeping his promise, as some understand slowness. Instead he is patient with you, not wanting anyone to perish, but everyone to come to repentance.
10 But the day of the Lord will come like a thief. The heavens will disappear with a roar; the elements will be destroyed by fire, and the earth and everything done in it will be laid bare. 11 Since everything will be destroyed in this way, what kind of people ought you to be? You ought to live holy and godly lives 12 as you look forward to the day of God and speed its coming. That day will bring about the destruction of the heavens by fire, and the elements will melt in the heat. 13 But in keeping with his promise we are looking forward to a new heaven and a new earth, where righteousness dwells.
14 So then, dear friends, since you are looking forward to this, make every effort to be found spotless, blameless and at peace with him. 15 Bear in mind that our Lord's patience means salvation, just as our dear brother Paul also wrote you with the wisdom that God gave him. 16 He writes the same way in all his letters, speaking in them of these matters. His letters contain some things that are hard to understand, which ignorant and unstable people distort, as they do the other Scriptures, to their own destruction. 17 Therefore, dear friends, since you have been forewarned, be on your guard so that you may not be carried away by the error of the lawless and fall from your secure position. 18 But grow in the grace and knowledge of our Lord and Savior Jesus Christ. To him be glory both now and forever! Amen (2 Peter 3:8-18 NIV)."

For His glory, and His alone. God bless.

References

1. According to UNICEF data, there are 1.3 billion adolescents in the world. This compares with a total population of 2.4 billion children and adolescents under the age of 18 in 2023, according to UNICEF's website June 4 2023.

2. Page 86 - Ouest France article: https://www.ouest-france.fr/societe/religions/de-plus-en-plus-de-chretiens-persecutes-dans-le-monde-6691061

3. Page 93 – US Department of Justice: https://www.ojp.gov/ncjrs/virtual-library/abstracts/legal-position-pedophiles

4. Page 94 - Nature Human Behaviour: https://www.nature.com/articles/s41562-023-01617-6.epdf?sharing_token=qCCs2OFKBDAf4sG2m-4AK9RgN0jAjWel9jnR3ZoTv0Pp6WiL6o0rsAZrTmzL_UN0RjM7oHAvV5vR55x3Wh_YbCWM-sDby_NFR_tJzpiI6zmEaxC4Xq5w6w3JSS8P9Fej9J-7HMagZDPwbMYoEv-W4iyq8VrKm9dSz2Q8T7kxFJ0GsscHN3AiFnErHTocSTrFgebNGLi0BlsgxtlLTCx_Ms7b2e5YHNpUF_zosG6K32g%3D&tracking_referrer=edition.cnn.com

www.ingramcontent.com/pod-product-compliance
Lightning Source LLC
LaVergne TN
LVHW010107170826
845678LV00012B/2273
9786501061726